Praise for *Understanding and Applying Value-Added Assessment: Eliminating Business Process Waste*

This book is mandatory reading for managers in my company. It has already giving us a common language with which to examine our processes, a common standard of what is accomplished (and what is not) by a specific verb, and a common methodology for streamlining our processes to serve our customers better and cut costs.

Richard W. Ingman
President
Hoffman Engineering Company

I have found Bill Trischler's methodology not only the most comprehensive to use, but one that clients can readily understand and embrace. This makes it easier to get positive results along with significant paybacks in a shorter time frame.

James D. Jannes
Director, Consulting Services

Having studied all the popular process improvement and reengineering literature, this book by Bill Trischler has become our method of choice for two reasons: it is an easy to understand, common-sense approach, and the value-added, non–value-added definitions enable our clients to focus on areas where they can achieve significant process improvements.

Steven K. Bruns
Director of Research & Major Account Services
The Nickelsen Group
A Reynolds + Reynolds Business Solutions Partner

Bill Trischler's book on value-added assessment is an excellent departure from the typically anecdotal reads available on the subject (non–value-added). Many of us are looking for something more analytical and useful in our daily operational improvement initiatives. This book hits the bull's-eye.

R. Kenn Hartman
President
Dynamic Solution Associates

My 25 years of business experience supports the finding that approximately 70% of all process time is absorbed in non–value-added activity. Mr. Trischler's book serves as an excellent guide for the continuous journey that modern management faces in today's complex cross-functional environment where the key to true success lies in the continuous elimination of non–value-added activity resulting in an increase in ultimate value for both customers and stakeholders.

Michael J. Kearney
Executive Vice President, Operations
Advance Transformer Co.

This book gives new and very practical guidelines on:

- Needs of process stakeholders to be considered
- Structured language to describe business processes
- What adds value and what doesn't

Using it will improve the quality of your business process reengineering efforts.

Joseph H. Redding, CMC
Senior Vice President
H. B. Maynard and Co., Inc.
Productivity Solutions Consultants

Understanding and Applying Value-Added Assessment

Also available from ASQC Quality Press

Mapping Work Processes
Dianne Galloway

Business Process Improvement
H. James Harrington, Ernst & Young, L.L.P.

Quality Quotes
Hélio Gomes

Show Me: The Complete Guide to Storyboarding and Problem Solving
Harry I. Forsha

Show Me: Storyboard Workbook and Template
Harry I. Forsha

Making Training Work: How to Achieve Bottom-Line Results and Lasting Success
Berton H. Gunter

Integrating Reengineering with Total Quality
Joseph N. Kelada

Avoiding the Pitfalls of Total Quality
Charles C. Poirier and Steven J. Tokarz

The Change Agents' Handbook: A Survival Guide for Quality Improvement Champions
David W. Hutton

Learner First™ Process Management software
with Tennessee Associates International

To request a complimentary catalog of publications, call 800-248-1946.

Understanding and Applying Value-Added Assessment

Eliminating Business Process Waste

William E. Trischler

ASQC Quality Press
Milwaukee, Wisconsin

Understanding and Applying Value-Added Assessment: Eliminating Business Process Waste
William E. Trischler

Library of Congress Cataloging-in-Publication Data
Trischler, William E., 1939–
    Understanding and applying value-added assessment: eliminating
business process waste / William E. Trischler.
      p. cm.
    Includes bibliographical references and index.
    ISBN 0-87389-369-7 (alk. paper)
    1. Organizational effectiveness. 2. Industrial efficiency.
3. Cost effectiveness. 4. Value added.   I. Title.
HD58.9.T75   1996
658.15'52—dc20   96-8811
                                                CIP

10 9 8 7 6 5 4 3 2 1

ISBN 0-87389-369-7

Acquisitions Editor: Roger Holloway
Project Editor: Kelley Cardinal

ASQC Mission: To facillitate continuous improvement and increase customer satisfaction by identifying, communicating, and promoting the use of quality principles, concepts, and technologies; and thereby be recognized throughout the world as the leading authority on, and champion for, quality.

Attention: Schools and Corporations
ASQC Quality Press books, audiotapes, videotapes, and software are available at quantity discounts with bulk purchases for business, educational, or instructional use. For information, please contact ASQC Quality Press at 800-248-1946, or write to ASQC Quality Press, P.O. Box 3005, Milwaukee, WI 53201-3005.

For a free copy of the ASQC Quality Press Publications Catalog, including ASQC membership information, call 800-248-1946.

Printed in the United States of America

 Printed on acid-free paper

Quality Press
611 East Wisconsin Avenue
Milwaukee, Wisconsin 53202

Contents

Figures and Tables

Figures

Tables

Preface

Setting the Stage

It is becoming increasingly important for organizations to put a process environment in place.

The success of every organization today increasingly depends on its business processes being aligned with its strategy, mission, and goals. Further, each individual in the organization must understand the importance of his or her role in achieving these goals. Therefore, it is becoming more important that organizations put in place a process environment to help people manage the changes needed in the basic processes they use to accomplish their work.

Current practices for documenting and modeling business processes to accomplish this objective are severely lacking in their capacity to indicate when change is actually required. Establishing such a control mechanism is much more complex than simply drawing flowcharts, capturing related policies, procedures, and work instructions in a word processor, and then stuffing all of it into a notebook that ends up collecting dust.

Value of Process Information

The underlying value of process information lies in its capacity to communicate a common understanding of how the business works, from such diverse abstractions as the strategic planning process engaged by senior management, to the well-defined steps taken by a machine operator cutting a piece of sheet metal on the shop floor.

In each instance, the information's value is only as good as the organization's ability to rapidly adapt its processes to changes in customer, business, or management requirements. It is well documented that such changes can only be accomplished through continuous analysis and improvement of the business processes.

Robust Solutions Are Needed

An architecture that supports the requirements of all stakeholders is needed.

To support the rapidly changing information needs of business, robust solutions are needed to help managers direct the extensive enterprisewide information environment. In developing these solutions, however, care must be taken to provide the process-oriented view without diminishing the value of information provided to support the distinct needs of each function.

Many organizations have been using business process models, developed in a process improvement environment, to fill the role of an enterprise's information architecture, which is intended to support the needs of all stakeholders. In fact, business process models are becoming the mechanism through which management directs changes in the business environment on an ongoing basis.

To improve the process of developing these information models, it is crucial that managers become much more aggressive in carefully analyzing and documenting current business processes. Adopting the value-added assessment techniques described in this book, combined with a standard process mapping methodology, is an excellent way to begin understanding the systemic processes necessary for an effective and reliable change management system.

Acknowledgments

A great many people made important contributions to the writing of this book, and I wish to thank all of them for their encouragement and support during its development and delivery.

First, my clients who keep my feet firmly on the ground by furnishing me with a continuous consignment of systemic issues to ponder and practical problems to solve. Their willingness to be guinea pigs for my novel experiments with new management methods is truly appreciated. I want to particularly thank Zack Lemelle of Ortho-McNeil Pharmaceutical; Ron Myers of Robinson Industries; John Knight of The Fabri-Form Company; Ed Condrick of Westinghouse; Ray Jonaitis of Little Tikes; Steven Bruns of The Nickelsen Group; Carlton Holley of SPIRC; Kenn Hartman of Dynamic Solution Associates; Jim Jannes of Daxus; and Joseph Redding of H. B. Maynard, as well as numerous others who prefer to remain nameless. Their contributions to the development and testing of the methods and techniques presented in this book have been priceless.

Second, my colleagues and coworkers at The MIRUS Group, particularly Ralph Osborne, Bill Stump, Frank DiVito, Tom Purvis, Chris Young, Bob Namestka, Clair John, and Barry Rack, who not only share the vision of developing more effective ways to manage business activities through process management, but also cherish the occupation of educating our client managers in the new methods and techniques being developed. Their commitment to finding practical solutions to complex management problems over the past five years has been thoroughly enjoyable. They were true collaborators in this project from beginning to end.

Finally, I thank my wife Juliann for her help and encouragement throughout the entire effort. Through long hours and sequestered weekends, she remained cheerful, good-natured, and helpful. I could not have written this book without her advice and guidance.

How to Use This Book

Value-Added in Perspective

Distinguishing between real and business value-added activities, and non–value-added activities, requires a sorting out process referred to as a *value-added assessment*.

This is not easy, nor is it an exact science. It involves a great deal of judgment, hence the need for a structure to apply when judging which activities add value and which do not. This is most important if you are benchmarking other companies, especially when they are not in the same business as your company. This document supplies the structure needed to implement a sound value-added assessment program.

A value-added assessment program is an essential tool for improving the effectiveness and efficiency of business processes. This is true whether the goal is to make a fundamental change in the way business is conducted or to solve a nagging operational problem.

Based on the experience of one consulting group,* as much as 60 percent to 80 percent of all process time is devoted to activities that do not add value for anyone. As Figure 0.1 shows, in the analysis phase of a project when planning time is minimal and little attention is paid to finding and eliminating non–value-added activities, both the time required to execute, review, and adapt the analysis process and the non–value-added content of the process increase.

Figure 0.2 shows that when planning time is sufficient and the techniques explained in this book are applied, both the time required to execute, review, and adapt an analysis process, and the non–value-added content of the process, are significantly reduced.

---

*Charlene B. Adari and Bruce A. Murray, *Breakthrough Process Redesign: New Pathways to Customer Value* (New York: AMACOM, 1994), 118.

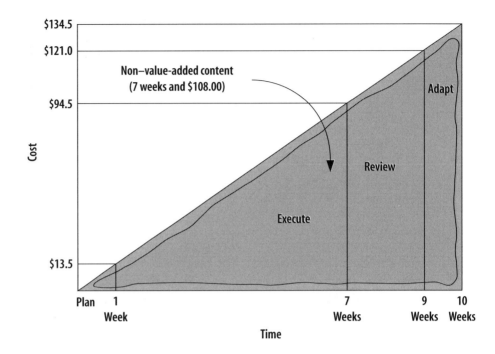

Figure 0.1. Process analysis phase (typical cost-time profile).

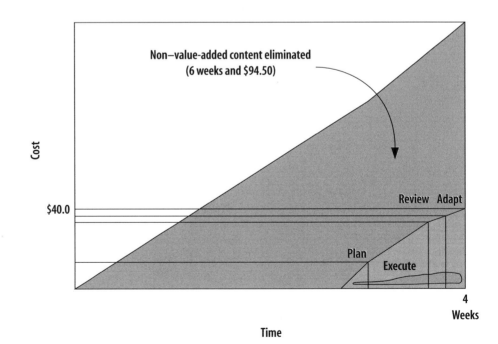

Figure 0.2: Process analysis phase (improved cost-time profile).

Process Improvement Project Cycle

Most process improvement projects are planned and managed through three specific phases—process analysis, design, and implementation. Table 0.1 shows the distribution of project time spent in each phase.*

Although very little empirical data exist, I believe that the improvement numbers shown on Figure 0.2 for the process analysis phase of a project can be extrapolated to the other two phases of a process improvement project: process design and implementation. As shown in Table 0.1, the savings in time and money are very impressive by any standard.

This book is designed to help process improvement analysts find and eliminate non–value-added steps in business processes. By doing so, significant savings in time and money are possible.

Book Structure

The business stakeholders chapter describes

- Eight groups of business stakeholders
- The basis for determining stakeholder value and their responsibilities and expectations
- Management's changing role in balancing *all* stakeholders' needs

Table 0.1: Distribution of project time by phase.

Project phase	Percent of time	"As is" Time	"As is" Cost	"To be" Time	"To be" Cost
Analysis	25.0%	10 weeks	$134,500	4 weeks	$40,000
Design	12.5%	5 weeks	67,250	2 weeks	20,000
Implementation	62.5%	25 weeks	336,250	10 weeks	100,000
Total	100.0%	40 weeks	$538,000	16 weeks	$160,000
Process improvement				60%	70%

*Ralph L. Osborne, *Process Improvement Project Effectiveness Study* (Pittsburgh, Pa.: The MIRUS Group, 1994), 6–7.

The business processes chapter describes

- The relationship between physical and business processes
- The three fundamentals of a well-designed process—effectiveness, efficiency, and flexibility

The business process evolution chapter discusses the need for both functional- and process-oriented organization to deal with the complexity that comes from growth and with isolation from stakeholders.

The methods for improving processes chapter emphasizes the two common objectives of any process improvement method.

1. Maximizing use of the organization's assets
2. Minimizing or eliminating waste

The chapter also describes value-added assessment and a process mapping technique that simplifies the task of documenting processes.

The process analysis phase chapter describes the six steps of the first phase of process improvement—analysis.

1. Defining business processes
2. Gathering stakeholder requirements
3. Preparing an as-is diagram
4. Preparing the process documentation
5. Verifying the as-is diagram
6. Performing the value-added assessment

The framework for analysis chapter describes four categories for classifying actions: plan, execute, review and adapt, and presents value-added and non–value-added examples for each category. This chapter introduces the actions or verbs that are included in the NVA dictionary.

The value-added assessment process chapter describes the multiple steps and paths of the assessment process, beginning with identifying business objectives and the process stakeholder(s).

The process time and cost elements chapter presents a detailed method for calculating the time and cost associated with a process—the final step in value-added assessment. The calculation methods are described for both low and high levels of abstraction in the process.

The NVA dictionary presents those actions or verbs that emerged most often in analysis as being potentially non–value-added. Definitions, examples, the rationale for their classification as non–value-added, synonyms, and so on are included. Directions for using the dictionary precede the list of 35 terms.

CHAPTER 1

Business Stakeholders

Who Are the Stakeholders?

Every business enterprise has at least eight stakeholder groups, whose concerns must be considered when analyzing business processes: customers, suppliers, managers, employees, creditors, investors, governments, and community groups.*

All stakeholders are important to the business.

A stakeholder is a person or group who has an interest in or benefits from the outputs of a business. All stakeholders are important to the business because they play a contributing, although sometimes conflicting role in the organization's success.

Of course, not all stakeholders participate in every process. Therefore, it is important to understand, as early in a process analysis project as possible, which stakeholders participate in the process. Having this information helps an improvement team avoid confusion about the purpose of the process and gets it quickly focused on stakeholders' needs.

---

*The ISO 9000 series standards suggest that there are five principal groups of stakeholders. The categories used here split out creditors and investors from owners; governments and communities from society; and managers from employees. See ANSI/ISO/ASQC Q9000-1-1994, page 2.

Balancing Stakeholder Needs

Balancing stakeholder needs is a fundamental responsibility of managers.

It is natural to assume that the most important stakeholder is the customer. In fact, over the past 10 years, many pundits of the quality movement suggested that the focus of everyone's attention should be exclusively on customer needs. The idea, however, was often confused by the use of such terms as *internal* and *external customer*—oftentimes to the exclusion of everyone else's needs.

Managers are now beginning to realize that customer needs are often in conflict with the suppliers of the things necessary to conduct a profitable business. As proposed by Figure 1.1, balancing the needs of all the stakeholders—given available resources—is one of managers' fundamental responsibilities. In other words, management's growing challenge is to structure the organization so that all stakeholders are recognized for their contribution to the success of the business—including management's own contribution.

For example, arbitrarily reducing the price of a product to satisfy competitive pressure, without due concern for other options, will certainly benefit customers in the short run. It will probably, however, harm several other stakeholder groups in the process.

If profitability is reduced because sales volume did not increase with the price reduction, investors will get nervous about the company's future earnings. To satisfy the investors, management may have to lay off employees or reduce the company's participation in community programs to reduce costs.

Understanding and satisfying each group's needs—that is, balancing their needs—without jeopardizing the others' well-being is an important determinant of whether or not an activity adds value to the company's value chain. Similarly, ignoring the needs of one group in favor of another's will

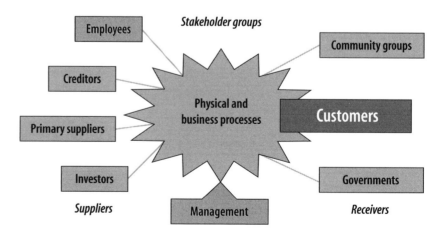

Figure 1.1: Managers balance stakeholders' needs.

seriously and adversely harm everyone's interests. In the end, the success of the entire business will suffer.

What Is Stakeholder Value?

Value is the perceived balance between the things people receive in exchange for the things they must give up to get them.

Stakeholder value is a very complex and misunderstood concept. It is not simply the price the customer pays for a product, the quality of the product received, the convenience of dealing with a supplier, meeting creditor obligations, satisfying employee needs, or maintaining the company's image. For most people, value includes all of those factors and much more. It is the perceived balance between the things people receive in exchange for the things they must give up to get them. For example, which restaurant delivers more value to the customer for the price of a meal?

> A four-star restaurant with superior food, an extensive wine list, a live piano player, romantic atmosphere, attentive service, and premium prices

or

> A fast-food restaurant with a limited menu, inexpensive prices, sterile and functional decor, and drive-through service.

The restaurant that delivers the most value depends completely on customers' expectations or their perception of value. If customers want a fast, inexpensive place to take the whole family for dinner, the fast-food restaurant will be chosen. If the dinner is for a very special person, then the four-star restaurant will probably be chosen. In either case, the restaurant has the opportunity to deliver the value customers expect.

Stakeholder Responsibilities

Each stakeholder group has a specific role to play in the success of the business. When customers buy the company's product or service at a specific price, they are paying for everything management believed it must do to get the product to market. Hopefully, customers will be satisfied with what they are buying.

Each stakeholder group has a specific role to play in the success of the business.

Management's role in the transaction is to make sure that customers are satisfied. Managers do this by making sure the product or service is provided in the most effective and cost-efficient way possible.

The basic role of primary suppliers is to provide needed components or service on time and at competitive prices. Management's role is to clearly communicate its requirements to the primary suppliers so that they can meet the company's requirements. In this instance, management is the customer.

An employee's role is to learn the job assigned and to perform it as well as possible. For his or her labor, the employee receives a salary and benefits commensurate with the difficulty of the task and the skills brought to the job. Management's role is to make sure the employee is provided with all the things—methods, procedures, and tools—necessary to perform the assigned job and to provide an appropriate work environment.

If management does not properly balance the cost of its products with the price received for them, it may be necessary to find a way to temporarily make up the difference. That is, management must find additional creditors or investors to supply the working capital needed to tide the company over until profitability returns.

The fundamental role of creditors—after reaching agreement on terms and conditions for the loan—is to make sure the funds are available to the company on a timely basis so that it does not risk losing its customers. For the use of the creditor's money, management's responsibility is to profitably operate the business so that the loans can be repaid when due.

Typically, investors are not directly involved in the operation of the business. Therefore, they are not very interested in how it is managed on a day-to-day basis. Once they are satisfied that the company has the right management, is in the right markets, and has the ability to earn a fair return, the investors' role is to step back and let management run the business without interference. If management is unable to earn a proper return for the investors, it will no doubt be replaced.

Management must find a way to determine the proper balance of the things each group receives.

Local, state, and federal governments, and community groups such as nonprofit associations and special interest groups, are organizations formed to deal with the interests of society in general. Traditionally, they have had a significant influence on business activities. Of course, the community as a whole can benefit or suffer based on the economic well-being of an industry. The steel industry is an excellent example.

Being good citizens—by volunteering for fund-raising events, speaking engagements, or teaching assignments—has always been an important role for managers. And it goes without saying that businesses have an obligation to pay their share of taxes in the jurisdiction where they do business.

Advances in communications technology have given various governments and community groups increased access to information about how companies are being operated—both good and bad. Often the information is used to support public concerns over several important community issues, such as the environment, product liability, and taxes. Management's role is to comply with the laws that apply to the business, and to encourage its employees to voluntarily contribute their time and expertise to community projects.

For management to provide value to all of the business stakeholders, it must find a way to determine the proper balance of the things each group receives. The following sections outline what each group expects in exchange for the price paid: customers, for the product or service they buy; primary suppliers and employees, for the products or services they supply to the company; creditors and investors, for the money they loan to or invest in the company; governments and community groups, for the sharing of the company's wealth and talents with society in general.

Customer Expectations

For customers, expected value is usually defined by the market availability of products in general and competing products in particular. In evaluating an automobile repair service, for example, customers usually do not compare one repair service to another. They compare it to the service received from a nonrelated business such as a fast-food restaurant. This may be one reason why customers are so often frustrated with repair services.

For customers, expected value is usually defined by the market availablity of products in general and competing products in particular.

For the person seeking excellent service, the whole experience at a fast-food store is generally pretty good. The things received for a reasonable price—fast service, consistent quality, and a friendly smile—keep customers coming back.

This same reasoning applies to most other businesses as well. As a general rule, customers will pay a fair price for a product or service if the following attributes are present.

- Perceived quality
- Variety of choices
- Transaction convenience
- Friendly service
- Prompt delivery
- Quick resolution of problems

At one point or another, everyone plays the role of both customer and supplier. For example, employees provide a company with their education, skills, and time—as suppliers. On the other hand, employees may consume the products or services further down the supply chain—as customers.

Therefore, it is not surprising that the expectations of various stakeholders are more or less equivalent. When analyzing each group, the differences that do emerge are simply the result of people playing different roles.*

---

*Given human nature, roles and relationships are really not that simple. When economic and political power enter into the equation, the situation definitely becomes much more complex. The point is that the roles people play in the business must be understood in relation to the methods, systems, and organizational structure established by management. That is really the only way roles can be changed.

Primary Supplier Expectations

The nature of the relationship between a company and its primary suppliers can have a significant impact on how well the business performs. Primary suppliers are organizations that supply the basic materials or services converted in the physical process. For example, if the relationship is a hostile one, the time and cost of doing business together will significantly increase. If a true partnership develops—where each party equally contributes to the relationship—the dealings can be jointly planned to prevent unproductive time and cost from creeping into the process.

When this kind of environment is cultivated, all stakeholder groups will benefit from a smooth-running operation with low costs. The kinds of things primary suppliers expect to gain from a mutual partnership with its customer are as follows:

- Fair price
- Repeat orders
- On-time payment
- Transaction convenience
- Open, honest communications
- Quick problem resolution
- Uniform dealings

The processes established to support the primary supplier relationship should incorporate all of these factors. For example, it is popular to conduct supplier audits—a potentially non–value-added and adversarial activity—to ensure that the supplier meets obvious customer stipulations.

If the customer establishes the audit criteria unilaterally, then it is certainly likely that a number of the supplier expectations will be forgotten. Perhaps a better approach is to include the supplier in the customer's process from the beginning and eliminate the need for the audit altogether.

Employee Expectations

Employees have been, and for the foreseeable future will continue to be, the backbone of work processes. A sorting-out process is taking place, however, where repetitive work done by people is gradually being replaced by advanced computer systems.

As the number of problems new technology solves increases, more low-level positions will be eliminated. Employees who are displaced will be compelled to learn new skills or exit from the workforce. It is likely that this trend will continue until all repetitive work is transferred to automated systems.

When this transformation is complete, the people remaining will be involved in the creative aspects of business—such as product design and process management. Employees who are able to adapt to the new environment will expect the same things that employees have always needed. This includes the following:

- Challenging work
- Job security
- Career advancement
- Competitive salary and benefits
- Healthy work environment
- Open, honest communications
- Balanced family and work life

As process management concepts and techniques are adopted, nonmanagement employees will increase their proficiency in performing the kinds of abstract tasks, such as planning, measurement, and control, that were previously performed by middle managers. Hopefully, this trend will provide employees greater control over their working conditions and lead to greater job satisfaction. Thus, employees will be empowered.

Creditor Expectations

Meeting creditor expectations is extremely important for those companies that use this source of funding.

Management is the primary contact with creditors—the people who lend the company money. The processes established to meet creditors' expectations are directed at accounting for the repayment of loans.

Although creditors usually play a very small role in the day-to-day operations of the business, meeting their expectations is extremely important for those companies that use this source of funding. Some of the important things creditors expect are as follows:

- On-time repayment of loans
- Open, honest communications
- Accurate, timely reporting
- Good employee relations
- Competent management

A creditor may put conditions on the business that ostensibly hinder management's flexibility in other areas of the business. For example, a creditor may stipulate a financial restriction that requires management to maintain a certain level of working capital or a specific working capital ratio. This restriction may cause the company to lose a strategic acquisition if the purchase price causes the target ratio to be exceeded. In the long run, acquiring the scarce resource may have given the company a competitive advantage that was not available elsewhere.

Once again, it is management's responsibility to make sure that creditors' needs are properly met. Also, for the benefit of other stakeholders, management must find another way to acquire scarce resources.

Investor Expectations

Although investors' expectations are primarily concerned with the company's financial performance, most investors know that the roads to market and earnings growth come through good management. And good management requires attaining a proper balance among the needs of all stakeholders.

Investors know that the roads to market and earnings growth come through good management.

Specifically, investors expect the following things for the money invested in a business.

- Excellent management
- Increased market value
- Open, honest communications
- Earnings growth
- Consistent dividends—if any
- Accurate financial records
- Responsiveness to questions and concerns

When a company's stock is publicly traded, the impact of poor management is often met by a sell-off of the company's stock. This, in turn, causes a reduction in the stock's market value. The action taken by creditors in reaction to the loss of stockholder confidence may be a reduction in the company's credit rating, thus making it more difficult to obtain working capital or to sell additional stock.

Taking this scenario further, if the company cannot raise the funds it needs, the business will decline as customers begin to buy competitors' products. Then employees are laid off to cut costs, and, in the end, everyone suffers. So although there does not seem to be a direct link between the customer who buys the product and an investor who provides working capital funds, one certainly affects the other if management does not properly direct its processes.

Government Expectations

Governments, at several levels in society, are responsible for providing services to the community where it is impractical or too expensive to provide them any other way. Funding for these services comes from collecting taxes imposed on citizens.

Governments expect compliance with the laws and all taxes paid on time.

Government officials, who are charged with carrying out the wishes of the people, establish the laws and operate the organizations that collect the taxes raised by enforcing the laws. Governments' expectations, with regard to business organizations in general, are as follows:

- Prompt payment of fees and taxes
- Prompt filing of reports
- Open reviews and inspections
- Conformity with laws and regulations
- Effective mandated services

Management's responsibility is to make sure that its employees comply with the laws while they are on company business, and that all taxes are paid on time. Of course, it is important that management establish the processes needed to make sure that the taxes paid are what they should be—no more and no less.

If management defaults on its duty to pay taxes, the government has the right to attach its property. If this occurs, then other stakeholders' interests—customers, suppliers, employees, creditors, and investors—are in jeopardy until the taxes can be paid.

The same predicament would exist if management decides to engage in illegal behavior. For example, if competing companies came together to fix the price of their products, which violates antitrust laws, management would be held accountable to the other stakeholders.

Community Expectations

Community leaders expect members of local companies to participate in the affairs of the community.

The involvement of management in local community affairs is usually voluntary, but one that historically has been good for all concerned. The people who are employed by a company are also members of the community, so they have an interest in making sure that joint community–company concerns and expectations are being disposed of in a systematic way.

Community leaders expect members of local companies to participate in the affairs of the community by doing the following:

- Adhere to laws and regulations.

- Conduct open, honest communication.
- Provide funds for community projects.
- Answer community questions promptly.
- Act quickly on community concerns.

The interest in participating in community activities is not equally divided among all types of businesses. Consumer companies, such as restaurants, television and radio stations, retail stores, and health service organizations, which generally have great visibility in the community, often join with community leaders to provide cultural services that are not available elsewhere.

On the other hand, participation by business-to-business suppliers, such as manufacturers, distributors, and consultants, tends to be on an individual-by-individual basis. In either case, it is important that management establish a working relationship with community leaders so that the interests of the community are an active element in the company's business plans.

Management Expectations

Management must be the interpreter and intermediary between the various stakeholder groups.

Stakeholders seldom come into direct contact with each other, so management must play a pivotal role in developing the processes required to balance their needs. The contradiction is that each group has its own idea of how things should be done, and management must be the interpreter and intermediary between the various groups. This is definitely a catch-22 situation.

How well management performs these tasks also has an impact on stakeholders. Managers have a significant stake in the business and expect to receive the following things in return for their time and effort.

- Challenging position
- Responsibility and authority (power)
- Rewards for performance
- Career advancement opportunities
- Competitive salary and benefits
- Open, honest communications

Historically, large companies have created several layers of management to plan, direct, and control day-to-day activities. Because of advancements in the use of computer technology, companies are now downsizing to reduce cost and push more control as far down the organization structure as possible.

Although the reduction is often implemented abruptly, middle managers are gradually being replaced by information systems that are more effective at doing the things these managers used to do—analyzing, controlling, and reporting. As a result, the traditional managerial role is changing significantly.

Management's Changing Role

The manager's role is rapidly changing.

The change in management's role has had a significant impact on how business is conducted over the past 10 years. Formerly, the manager was an advocate and champion for customers, a father or mother figure to employees and their families, a saint to suppliers of goods and services, a watchdog for creditors, a guardian angel to investors, a bill collector for governments, and an omnipotent being to community groups. To manage all of these perceived responsibilities, a command-and-control structure was perfected; policies and procedures were developed that restricted everyone's movements and dampened creativity; and an endless supply of managers were hired to manage and control the whole mess.

Now, the manager's role is rapidly changing. With the introduction of new methods and technology, companies are reducing the management structures, turning more responsibility and authority over to employees, and assigning the remaining managers the new roles of educator and coach. New terms such as *learning organization* and *systemic processes** are gaining popularity in progressive companies.

The developing concept of process management can also be used to refocus management's attention toward finding the proper balance among methods, structure, people, and culture. To initiate the change process, managers must be willing to experiment with these new concepts. At the pace that technology is changing, the time required to make an orderly transformation to the new methods is running short.

Final Thought

Understanding each stakeholder's needs and the interaction between each of the stakeholder groups is important for the project team to understand. Thus, a thorough analysis of the data collected for each stakeholder should provide a complete picture of what management needs to do to satisfy all stakeholders' needs. Completing this kind of analysis is an absolute prerequisite to starting the process analysis phase of any process improvement project.

---

*Peter Senge, *The Fifth Discipline: The Art and Practice of the Learning Organization* (New York: Doubleday, 1990).

Chapter 2

Business Processes

Physical and Business Process Basics

Figure 2.1 shows a realistic model that illustrates the relationship of business processes and physical processes. Basically, both process and discrete processes are physical activities that convert raw materials to finished products.

The output of a physical process can be either a tangible product, such as an automobile, radio, TV, or computer, or an intangible service, such as medical, legal, or financial advice. Physical processes are essentially linear because the steps can be well defined, and they progress from beginning to end in a fairly straightforward manner.

As shown in Figure 2.1, physical (or linear) processes (light gray color) deal with activities that are repetitive and done step-by-step, such as in a product assembly line, a high-volume paperwork process, or a continuous manufacturing process. The foremost characteristic of physical work is that each step can be specified in advance. For example, if step 1 is made up of three substeps and always goes before step 2, which has five substeps, then they are all definable and repetitious. To improve a physical work process, a process management team (PMT)* looks for errors early in the sequence that may be causing most of the problems later in the process.

---

*This kind of team is sometimes referred to as a *process improvement team* (PIT), a group of six to eight people assigned to analyze and recommend improvement in a process.

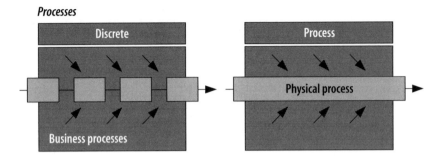

Figure 2.1:   Business vs. physical processes.

Business processes are a mixture of both linear and nonlinear work.

On the other hand, business processes are a mixture of both linear and nonlinear work. The objective of these processes is not only to support the physical conversion process, but also to meet the other requirements of running a business, such as paying employees, reporting to a board of directors, and so on.

Business processes convert conceptual input into a tangible output.

In the simplest terms, business processes convert conceptual input into a tangible output—a report, document, or plan—that provides guidance, control, or information about the health of the business. The principle for designing and implementing a business process is to ensure the effective and efficient use of the organization's resources.

Nonlinear work consists of individual steps that can usually be done in parallel, detached from each other, or in a variety of sequences. Often future activities cannot be determined until some of the results from the current activity are known. This is particularly true when new or untried methods, procedures, or products are being developed and implemented.

For example, the patterns of decisions leading to the development of a new product or packaging method in a pharmaceutical company are designed to ensure the success of the final product in the marketplace. To achieve this goal, the PMT should look for ways to get the required perspectives—clinical, regulatory, and product management—as early in the process as possible to prevent critical failures later.

The distinction between linear and nonlinear activities sometimes clouds the value-added analysis. This is particularly true in large organizations where the work is a blend of both types of processes, such as managing facilities divisions. In such cases, the analysis must be applied at the lowest level in the process, where appropriate.

Designing Business Processes

The primary design objective is to perform the process better, faster, and cheaper.

The primary objective in business process design is to create a process that meets the stakeholder's requirements better, faster, and cheaper than competitors can with their design. When the organization achieves this objective, then all stakeholders profit from the results.

For example, customers will benefit through lower prices, higher quality, and improved customer service. Employees benefit through better working conditions, competitive pay, and greater job security. Investors benefit through a greater return on their investment. And management achieves greater flexibility in balancing the needs of all stakeholders as business conditions change.

Therefore, the objective in designing—or redesigning—a process is to make sure the conversion of input to output is done as efficiently and flexibly as possible so that everyone benefits. A well-designed process has an additional benefit to the business because it lessens the adverse impact of cross-functional issues, those which have the potential of invading or interrupting the natural flow of the critical systemic processes.*

Process Effectiveness, Efficiency, and Flexibility

The three fundamental elements of a well-designed process are its effectiveness, efficiency, and flexibility. If these elements are balanced, maximum results will be achieved from the process.

To be effective, the output from the process must satisfy one or more of the business's objectives while meeting or exceeding the recipient stakeholders' needs. If a process meets these requirements, it is viewed by most people as being a quality process, even through it may not be an efficient process. An example of an effective process is employees receiving their paychecks when expected, for the amount expected.

A process is efficient if the conversion of inputs to an output is done in the shortest time possible, with the lowest utilization of resources. That is, the cycle time required to produce error-free output is the lowest value possible.

It is very rare for a process to be flexible without being efficient and effective.

Of course, a process is not effective just because it is efficient, since the process may not be needed at all. An example of an efficient process is that employee paychecks are processed in the shortest time and at the lowest cost possible.

A process is flexible if it can adjust quickly and easily to changes in internal constraints, to poor input quality, or to changes in stakeholder requirement for services. When a process is flexible it can adapt to new requirements without significant modification to capital equipment, personnel, information systems, or facilities.

It is very rare for a process to be flexible without being efficient and effective; but the reverse is certainly true. An example of a flexible process is when the government modifies the tax rate, and the resulting changes in calculating pay can be made quickly and with a minimum number of changes to the process.

---

*The term *critical systemic processes* refers to the processes necessary to sustain the enterprise; for example, the customer order to fulfillment process.

Chapter 3

Business Process Evolution

Early Growth Stages

Most processes begin in an ad hoc way in response to a particular stakeholder need.

Organizations do not intend to have steps in their processes that do not add value for their stakeholders. In fact, most processes begin in an ad hoc way in response to a particular stakeholder need. Typically a process starts out being relatively simple, efficient, and performed by just a few individuals.

Because processes initially involve only a few people, they necessarily perform many different functions. As they learn more about what the stakeholder needs or how to do the job better, they continuously refine the process to improve it.

Despite management's best intentions, processes begin to lose effectiveness over time.

Further adjustments to the process occur as the organization, stakeholder requirements, or business environment change. These modifications usually introduce greater complexity and inefficiency into the process. Despite management's best intentions, the process begins to lose effectiveness over time.

As stakeholder demands continue to increase, more people are brought into the process. Usually they enter into the process component where bottlenecks exist or where expertise is missing. In an attempt to better manage the bottlenecks or lack of expertise, management hires new people who have training in a specific discipline or functional expertise. For example, to better sell its product to the customer, a company hires salespeople and

21

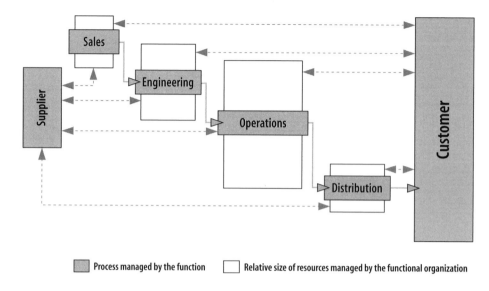

Figure 3.1: Functional-oriented organization.

forms a sales department. The organization begins to look and function like the process diagram shown in Figure 3.1.

Specific functions are created to deal with each area of expertise. Work begins to flow irregularly and in a waterfall manner where each function passes the work along when its tasks have been completed. Interaction with final customers becomes sporadic, and responsibility for meeting customers' needs is dispersed among the various functions. The end result is that the functions turn their focus toward resolving departmental problems, and nobody is responsible for addressing cross-functional issues.

Need for Functional-Oriented Organization

As a general rule, separate functions strive to perform their work as efficiently and effectively as possible. But often they improve the processes needed to support their own area of responsibility, unaware that they may be altering the effectiveness of other departments. For example, the work of accounts payable may improve, but inefficiencies in purchasing and receiving may result in the suboptimization of the complete process from the final customer's or supplier's point of view.

This occurs because a company often evaluates its department managers with performance factors appropriate to the function, but not necessarily consistent with the company's or other departments' objectives. For example, the materials management department is customarily responsible for lowering work-in-process inventory while manufacturing operations is charged with increasing machine utilization.

These metrics often result in a conflicting situation between the two departments since one way to improve machine utilization is to increase work-

Departmental objectives often result in conflicting cross-functional situations.

in-process inventory. And for those companies using full-absorption accounting, building inventory will incidentally produce an increase in short-term profits. The predictable consequence of each department striving to meet its own objectives at the other's expense is the creation of even more controls between the two departments to equalize the process flow once again.

Growth Adds Complexity

As a company grows, more steps are added to the process, making it more complex. As problems continue to occur, management institutes more controls. Unfortunately, the new controls are usually designed to correct process outputs, or to manage the poor quality of process inputs, instead of changing or correcting defects in the process itself. Even if the controls do work, they often remain long after the original problems have disappeared.

For example, in a bank or insurance company, applications or claims are examined by administrative clerks to make sure they are filled out correctly. If not, the form is returned to the applicant. Why doesn't anyone think about revising the form to make it easy for the applicant to fill out? Usually the clerks don't have the time to make the form easy, because they are too busy doing the examination work.

As a company continues to grow, people's jobs become increasingly dependent on the new controls. Managers react with an unwillingness to eliminate the controls without incentives because of the possibility of losing authority over the process or, in some cases, their own jobs.

Isolation from Stakeholders

In large organizations, most people are seldom in a position to directly talk to a stakeholder. Therefore, it is difficult for them to associate what they do with what the stakeholder desires. This situation is magnified in a functionally oriented organization because the people in one function generally have little contact with the people in another function—and management is the interpreter between them.

Departmental achievement is often forced inward toward performing non–value-added activities, such as coordinating, expediting, record keeping, and administration.

Consequently, a significant portion of the work performed does not really satisfy the internal, cross-functional requirements of any functional specialty. With a growing number of internal controls being placed on the functions, the focus of achievement is often forced inward toward performing non–value-added activities, such as coordinating, expediting, record keeping, and administration.

The Taylorism device often used to improve the efficiency of internal processes is to divide responsibilities into small, independent elements. When changes are necessary to respond to new requirements, such as a new competitive product or government regulation, however, the coordination of changes in the individual elements becomes extremely difficult. Thus, resistance to change increases.

Need for Process-Oriented Organization

Everyone's attention and efforts must be focused on the final output of the process.

In a process-oriented organization, management determines the needs of each stakeholder and establishes the necessary processes to meet those needs. The challenge, then, is to get everyone's attention and efforts focused on the final output of the process and away from furnishing non–value-added information to a functional manager.

Figure 3.2 shows how this refocusing would operate for at least two of the stakeholders of the prospect-proposal-to-payment process. The focus and attention of all the functional participants is toward the process and not internally toward the function.

In the process environment, one person becomes the process owner with the overall responsibility of insuring a smooth-running process. This includes providing the resources—people, machinery, and facilities—necessary to deliver the desired output.

Of course, having a process-oriented organization does not mean that the functional specialties are no longer important to the business. Indeed, their role is strengthened because the focus of their work takes on direct meaning to individual stakeholders.

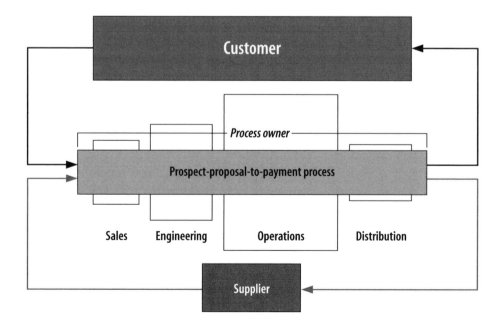

Figure 3.2: **Process-oriented organization.**

For example, in designing a product, the engineering department can now work in parallel with every other function that has input into the product design, including customers and suppliers. This is a concept referred to as concurrent engineering. Yet, the functions still have control over how they actually accomplish their work. For example, even in a concurrent engineering team environment, the engineering staff serves as a center of expertise for providing engineers with the knowledge, methods, procedures, and tools needed to perform their jobs. Of course, this same notion applies to all of the other functional specialties as well.

The primary difference between functional and process management is in the way work is organized and performed. The functional organization is focused on serving internal functions, while the process organization is focused on serving the process stakeholders.

Impact of Government Regulations

From time to time, federal, state, and local governments add new rules, regulations, or controls that affect how an organization operates, and over which management may have only limited control. In fact, most new regulations add a significant amount of paperwork to the business without even indirectly benefiting the nongovernment stakeholders.

Most new regulations add paperwork to the business without even indirectly benefiting the nongovernment stakeholders.

All regulations, however, require interpretation by someone in the organization. If the regulations are not interpreted properly, the unfavorable impact of added regulations will be significantly magnified, resulting in an unhealthy impact on the business. Therefore, care should be taken to ensure that the organization does not overreact to the needs of governmental agencies.

Chapter 4

Methods for Improving Processes

Methods and Tools

The best way to improve process efficiency, effectiveness, and flexibility is to adopt a well-organized methodology and consistently apply it over an extended period of time. Any one of the approaches shown in Table 4.1 could be used for this purpose. Of course, each method has its own set of strengths and weaknesses. Care should be taken to ensure that the one selected has the full support of management and that it is supported with appropriate employee training programs. More often than not, the method adopted is considerably less important than the need to train employees to consistently apply it over a long period of time.

Each of the methods shown in Table 4.1 approaches the issue of process improvement from a different point of view. What the methods have in common, however, is the objective of helping managers achieve the following results.

- Maximize the use of the organization's assets (capital, machinery, technology, and people).
  - —Improve responsiveness to the customer.
  - —Align people's skills to necessary tasks.

Table 4.1: Process improvement approaches.

Approach	Objective	Tools/Method
Activity-based costing	Cut cost.	Cost buildup over process/ value-added analysis
Process value analysis	Streamline a single process/ reduce cost and time.	Value analysis for each process step
Business process improvement	Continuously improve one or all processes in terms of cost, time, and quality.	Process step classification, quality tools.
Cycle time reduction	Reduce the time it takes to perform a process.	Process step analysis
Information engineering	Build a system along process lines.	Descriptions of current and future processes
Business process innovation	Use change levers to radically improve key processes.	Change levers, future vision

Source: Adapted and reprinted by permission of Harvard Business School Press. From *Process Innovation: Reengineering Work through Information Technology* by Thomas M. Davenport. Boston, MA 1993, p.142. Copyright © 1993 by Ernst & Young. All rights reserved.

—Increase the adaptability to changes in the business environment.

—Align information systems to the process being supported.

—Reduce costs.

—Provide the organization with a competitive advantage.[*]

- Minimize or eliminate waste due to the following causes.

    —Overproduction (inventory, interest charges, overhead, and paperwork)

    —Wait time (queues, delays, and decisions)

    —Transportation (handling and communication)

    —Processing waste (scrap, garbage, and waste)

    —Inventory (overstocking and obsolescence)

    —Motion (walking to obtain tools or information, picking up tools, and searching for information)

    —Product defects (rework and inspection)[†]

---

[*]H. James Harrington, *Business Process Improvement: The Breakthrough Strategy for Total Quality, Productivity, and Competitiveness* (New York: McGraw-Hill, 1991).
[†]Kiyoshi Suzaki, *The New Manufacturing Challenge: Techniques for Continuous Improvement* (New York: Free Press, 1987).

What Is a Value-Added Assessment?

An essential component of analyzing a business process is a technique called *value-added assessment* (VAA). VAA is a detailed examination of every step in a process to determine if it contributes to stakeholders' requirements or needs.

The objective of VAA is to optimize the value-added steps and minimize or eliminate non–value-added steps.

The objective of a VAA is to optimize the value-added steps and minimize or eliminate non–value-added steps. Analyzing process steps for added value is a key concept in most process improvement methods.

When properly combined with a dynamic process diagramming methodology, VAA techniques form an effective set of tools for achieving the aforementioned objective. The fact is that the VAA process described here is a fundamental component, even though from different origins, of the following methods: activity-based costing, process value analysis, continuous process improvement, and cycle time reduction. The other methods shown in Table 4.1, information engineering and business process innovation, could also benefit by integrating VAA techniques.

Information Engineering

The IE approach is not particularly concerned with whether or not the process is being performed in the best way possible.

Information engineering (IE) is one of the most commonly used techniques for analyzing the various dimensions of business processes. These dimensions include data, entity relationships, and data flow.

IE uses specific process and data models to find ways to improve information processes. The primary goal of the IE approach is to streamline a process by improving data flows and managing the interfaces among organizations.

Unfortunately, the IE approach is not particularly concerned with whether or not the process is being performed in the best way possible, or if it is needed in the first place.

IE can be augmented, however, by embracing VAA techniques. By locating and eliminating non–value-added steps, the information analyst could probably reduce the need for a significant amount of data requirements.

Business Process Reengineering

Radical change suggests a sharp learning curve coupled with a significant commitment of time and money.

Business process reengineering (BPR) suggests that the best approach to more useful processes is to make a radical, "clean slate" transformation without worrying about how things are currently done. Radical change, however, suggests a sharp learning curve coupled with a significant commitment of time and money. Frequently the path taken does not always lead to the best solution to the problem.

VAA can fulfill an important role by permitting a team to achieve small cycle-time reductions and cost gains.

Nevertheless, when conducting a BPR analysis, short-term improvements are usually identified that can be accomplished relatively simply and easily. These small, incremental improvements can certainly be made both before and after making the radical change. Thus, VAA can fulfill an important role by permitting a team to achieve small cycle-time reductions and cost gains prior to the BPR solution taking effect—and after the team has reached the next learning plateau.

Avoid Instant Solutions

In their book *Reengineering the Corporation,* * Hammer and Champy wrote that a business consists of a set of interrelated processes, and to understand the business one must understand the processes and their relationships. This notion implies that companies should be encouraged to manage processes differently than they have in the past—perhaps from a process, as opposed to functional, point of view.

Since the book was published, a proliferation of new fads claiming to effectively address the problems associated with designing and managing business processes has emerged. In fact, the number of new methodologies appearing in the market has increased at an exponential rate over the past three years. Just go to the business section of a well-stocked bookstore to see the number of books that profess "new and successful" methods for implementing business process engineering, cycle-time reduction, total quality management, or continuous process improvement.

Instant solutions tend to polarize functional departments.

The difficulty with these instant solutions is that they tend to polarize functional departments more than they already are. This kind of polarization often leads to disagreement as to who has the best methodology or technique to solve the organization's problems, perpetuating the not-invented-here syndrome.

Additionally, when the latest craze is brought to bear, it tends to divert management's attention away from sound business strategy. For example, if all organizations could perform the same tasks as quickly and easily as their competitors, they would do so. In the end, no one would really achieve an advantage or exceptional return on their efforts. This would be like a product pyramid scheme, in which only the original implementors win.

The time is right for results-minded managers to take control of their processes by energetically adopting process management methods and techniques. The notion of process management rests on the premise that a

*Michael Hammer and James Champy, *Reengineering the Corporation: A Manifesto for Business Revolution* (New York: HarperBusiness, a Division of HarperCollins Business, 1993).

The latest craze tends to divert management's attention away from sound business strategy.

set of generic concepts underlies every business activity. This set of concepts, which collectively are referred to as the process environment, are the underpinning of every BPR and process improvement methodology.

A fruitful process environment comes about by creating a culture that makes process management a meaningful part of the values and principles of everyone in the organization. The notion is supported and emphasized through the consistent application of a standard methodology that helps management accomplish the following objectives.

- Create processes that are linked to the strategies and priorities of the business.
- Get everyone in the organization focused on the right processes.
- Improve process effectiveness, efficiency, and flexibility so that the work is performed better, faster, and cheaper.

Process management is the underpinning of every business process reengineering and process improvement methodology.

By aligning everyone's work to the strategic goals, a better understanding of the core business processes can be developed. These processes can then be improved through better diagramming, documentation, and analysis methods. Further, management can ensure that the right processes are in place and operating properly by assigning process owners who can make the processes highly visible.

Labeling Non–Value-Added Activities (Actions)

"If you can see it, you can improve it.™*"*

In most process improvement methods, creating an as-is diagram is a prerequisite to analyzing a process. This task can be greatly simplified by using a simple sentence structure technique to label the steps on the as-is diagram. The technique is characterized as a *Resource-Action-Object*™ paradigm.

An example of its usage is shown in step 5 of Figure 4.1, "manufacturing (resource) produces (action) standard product (object)." The light gray color indicates that the step is value-added.*

When a project team creates the as-is diagram, some actions or verbs almost always indicate the existence of non–value-added work. For example, the task "accounting (resource) reviews (action) customer order (object)," step 3 in Figure 4.1, is colored rose to show that it is a non–value-added step.

---

*A simple practice for using color in a process diagram is: light gray for value-added steps; rose for non–value-added steps; dark gray for external entities; and medium gray for connector steps. Of course, any color scheme can be used.

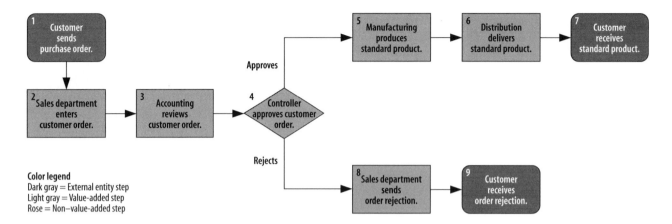

Figure 4.1: Process as-is diagram.

Coloring non–value-added steps in a striking color, such as rose or red, will help make them easily recognizable for further analysis. This is an application of the basic diagramming notion, "If you can see it, you can improve it.™"

When using color, the analyst should not be surprised if a majority of the steps on an as-is process diagram are colored rose or red, indicating non–value-added. In this particular diagram, four of the six internal process steps are rose while only two are light gray. This indicates that a significant amount of time and cost could be eliminated if the process were redesigned.

Chapter 5

Process Analysis Phase

A process improvement project typically advances through three distinct phases: process analysis, process design, and process implementation. Although the VAA technique can be used throughout all three phases, the main body of work takes place during the sixth step of the first phase, process analysis, as shown in Figure 5.1.

It is during this phase that enough information has been collected to determine whether or not a step in the process being studied provides value to its stakeholder. As Figure 5.1 shows, five important steps precede step 3.6, process management team conducts VAA. These five steps are data accumulation steps performed by the PMT* to document the scope of the project, create an as-is process diagram, collect supporting information, and confirm everyone's understanding of the process.

Customary data collection techniques, such as Post-it™ notes or packaging paper, can be used to record information in steps 1 through 5. It is recommended, however, that the data be captured electronically during the accumulation process to help ensure its homogeneity and manageability.

---

*In preparing this section of the guidebook, an assumption has been made that the process management team has been formed and this group is executing the process analysis steps. Of course, a process analyst can also perform these tasks.

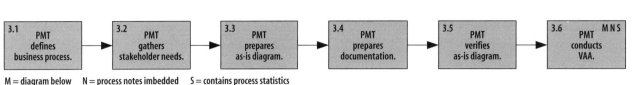

M = diagram below   N = process notes imbedded   S = contains process statistics

Figure 5.1: **Steps in process analysis phase.**

Since step 3.6 is the central focus of this book, it will be explored in greater detail in a later section. The intent is to drill down on this step to show the individual actions required to identify and document the non–value-added work in a process. The drill down will also illustrate how to calculate value-added time and cost. Before discussing it, however, the steps that precede it are explained.

Step 3.1 Team Defines Business Process

The kickoff step in the process analysis is to define the scope of the business process being examined and its relationship to other processes the organization uses to plan, execute, review, and adapt its behavior. The purpose of this step is to establish the scope of the process so that the PMT members are in agreement about the work to be accomplished. The process definition form shown in Figure 5.2 can be used to collect the key information. The process definition consists of the following elements. The letter preceding each category corresponds to those shown on the form.

Process Type

Definition: The process type is a classification system that will help the PMT gain an understanding of the scope and context of the process being studied. The model shown in Figure 5.3 is an example of a classification system for the high-level systemic processes that exist in a typical business.

These particular categories were developed in a brainstorming session for a manufacturing company, but it is relatively easy for an organization to develop its own high-level abstractions by using the affinity diagram technique to group low-level processes together and then name each of the major groups. The number of high-level processes for most businesses should not exceed six to eight.

Employing this kind of classification system will help coordinate the efforts of multiple projects and prevent conflicting project objectives. Additionally, it will help save a considerable amount of time during the analysis

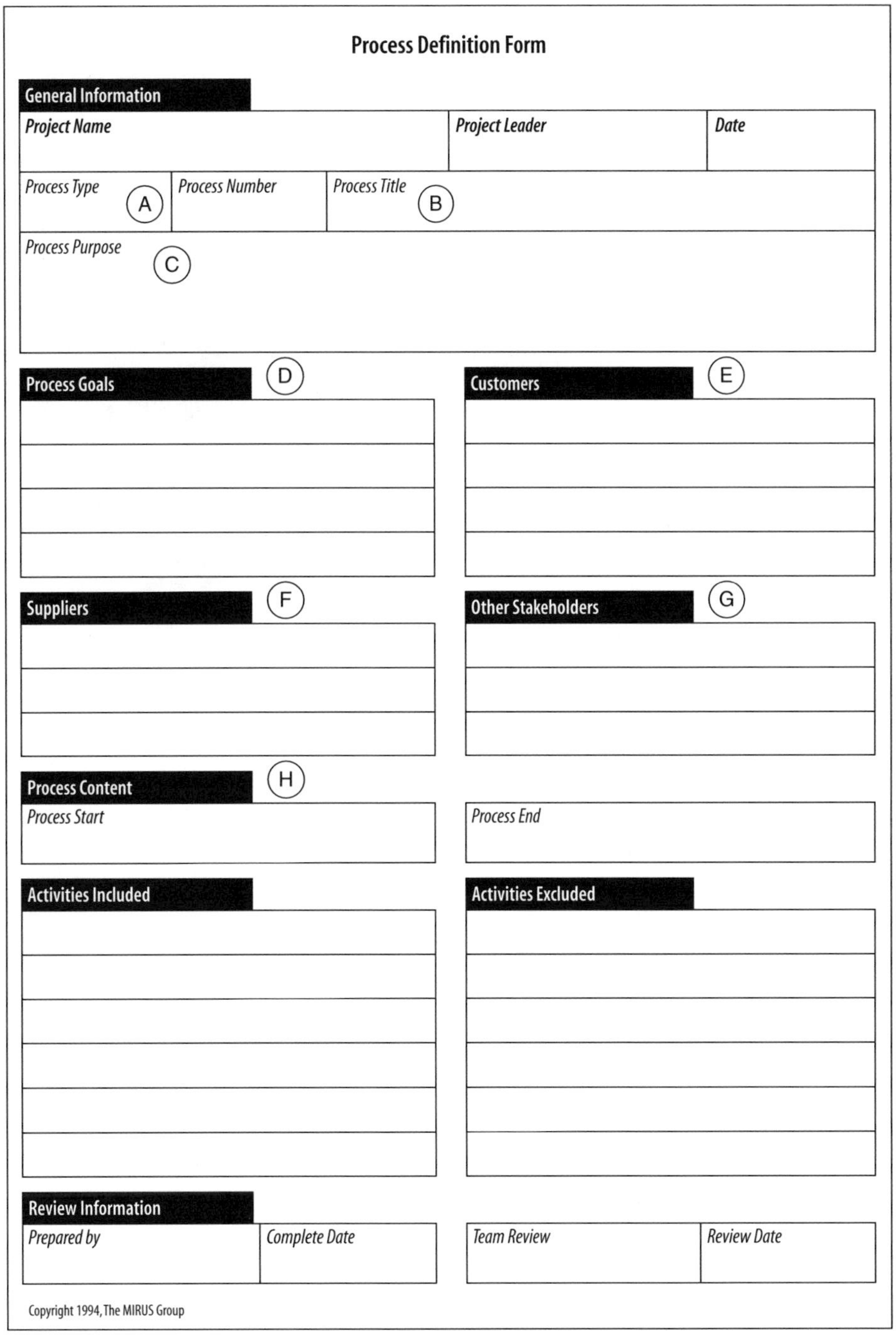

Process Definition Form

General Information

Project Name		Project Leader	Date

| Process Type (A) | Process Number | Process Title (B) | |

Process Purpose (C)

Process Goals (D)

Customers (E)

Suppliers (F)

Other Stakeholders (G)

Process Content (H)

Process Start	Process End

Activities Included

Activities Excluded

Review Information

Prepared by	Complete Date	Team Review	Review Date

Copyright 1994, The MIRUS Group

Figure 5.2: Process definition form.

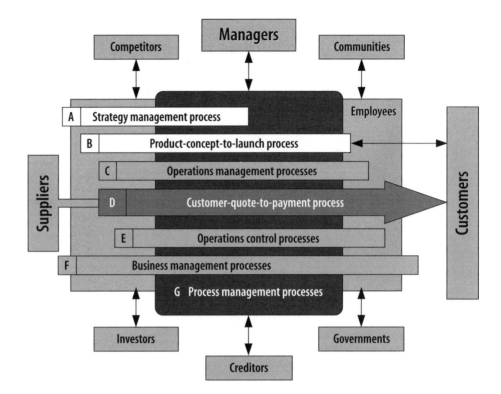

Figure 5.3: Business process model.

phase because process definitions can be coordinated and duplicating resources and objects will be minimized.

Example: The process type for the customer quote to delivery process is D because it falls within the scope of the customer-quote-to-payment category. In this instance, the scope of the process is rather broad and only excludes those activities related to ensuring that the customer pays for the product or service delivered.

Ⓑ Process Title

Definition: To help the PMT get focused, every process should have a unique name. Often it is difficult for PMT members to reach agreement on a name, but care should be taken to name the process so that it will last beyond the life of the project and be understood by everyone in the organization.

Example: Customer quote to delivery: This title gives a clear indication of the process scope.

(C) Process Purpose

Definition: The process purpose is a short statement of what the process intends to accomplish. The statement should be as concise as possible, and the PMT members should be in complete agreement with its intent. Care should be taken to make sure the statement indicates how the stakeholder benefits.

Example: Deliver assemblies to the customer's dock.

(D) Process Goals

Definition: The process goals are based on the customer or other stakeholder values and quantify the process purpose.

Example: Ninety percent of the orders received will be shipped to reach customers' docks within 48 hours of receipt.

(E) Customers

Definition: These are the stakeholder groups who receive the output of the process. The process content determines the stakeholders.

Example: Automobile manufacturers who use assemblies to produce cars for consumers.

(F) Suppliers

Definition: These are the stakeholder groups who provide input to the process. The process content determines the suppliers of the process.

Example: Raw material and parts companies

(G) Other Stakeholders

Definition: This is a person or group who stands to gain or lose based on the results of the process. Every process has stakeholders who are not directly involved in the work but who definitely have an interest in the work performed or the output. Identifying these people is important because they will likely be obstacles when implementing changes to the process.

Example: Department of Defense (external) and purchasing department (internal)

(H) Process Content

Definition: The process content identifies the boundaries of the process being analyzed. The boundaries define where the process starts and ends, and states what related activities are included and excluded from the analysis.

Process start

Definition:	This is the first step in the process. The input for this step always comes from sources external to the process.
Example:	Prospect submits request for quote (RFQ). The RFQ is an object that has specific attributes and characteristics.

Obtain a copy of all businesss documents—they are the vehicle for transporting information between functions.

Process end

Definition:	This is the last step in the process. The stakeholder (who receives the final output for this step) is always external to the process.
Example:	Customer accepts product delivery.

Activities included

Definition:	These are subprocesses of the customer quote to delivery that will be included on the process diagram.
Examples:	Quote preparation
	Order placement
	Scheduling
	Product manufacturing
	Product packing
	Shipping
	Product delivery

Activities excluded

Definition:	These activities provide input or accept output from the activities included on the diagram, but will not be included in any detail on the diagram.
Examples:	Ordering raw material
	Collecting accounts receivable
	Writing off bad debts

Step 3.2   Process Team Gathers Stakeholder Requirements

Evaluate the shareholder's entire experience with the company—not just with the process or service.

The second step in process analysis is to determine what the stakeholders examined in step 3.1 consider to be valuable. The information that the PMT collects will form the basis for identifying the process steps that add value and those that can be eliminated.

One of the most useful ways to gather information about a stakeholder's needs is through a survey. For example, a customer or employee survey is a common method for collecting views about specific issues. This kind of survey can also be adapted to collect the opinions of other stakeholder groups as well. Table 5.1 provides a list of the most common data collection methods used to document stakeholder needs.

Table 5.1:   Methods for gathering stakeholder information.

Method	Description	Comments	Stakeholder
Direct observation	Watch how and why people use product or service.	Effective for well-defined products or services in limited geographic area with limited survey population.	Customers Suppliers Employees
Focus groups	Facilitate small groups as members discuss values of importance to them.	Effective for fairly specific purposes and issues where a small sample of a large population is considered adequate because there is some diversity of needs and perceptions.	Customers Suppliers Employees Community groups
Face-to-face interviews	Guided face-to-face conversations.	Effective for detailed probing when a limited sample is acceptable or considerable time is available.	All
Telephone interviews	Scheduled, structured interviews by phone.	Effective for probing in depth when a large sample is necessary and the time is short or access is limited.	All
Written surveys	Structured written questioning.	Effective for volume response on well-defined issues. Useful for continuous monitoring, geographic diversity.	Customers Suppliers Employees Investors Community groups
User groups	Facilitated discussions of values by select users (or nonusers) at periodic intervals over a long time span.	Effective for probing in depth, building relationships to increase candor in feedback, and continuous monitoring.	Customers Suppliers Employees Community groups

PMT members must remain objective when collecting stakeholder information.

The most important issue to bear in mind when constructing a survey is that the investigation is aimed at evaluating the entire experience the stakeholder has with the company.* So survey questions should be constructed to explore the entire length of the process—and not just the output of the process.

For example, when evaluating a customer's needs, the survey should not only measure the actual use of the product or service, but it should also explore how employees treat the customer's questions or deal with his or her problems on a day-to-day basis. Additionally, whether the survey is submitted in writing or conducted in person, the PMT members must be careful not to inject their views of what the stakeholder's experience has been when interacting with the company. In fact, all of the conclusions reached from these surveys must be kept as objective as possible, or their value to the team will be limited.

Make sure that the stakeholder requirements are accurately communicated internally.

Internally focused processes provide outputs to other internal processes rather than directly to the ultimate stakeholder. For example, when processing a customer order, the sales department generally records the customer's requirements and passes them along to engineering, who is responsible for designing the product.

It is very important that the output of the order entry process clearly conveys the customer's needs so that engineering designs the product the customer really requested. The PMT should be constantly aware of the customers and suppliers of each process step.

Step 3.3 Process Team Prepares As-Is Diagram

The third step in process analysis is to create a process diagram showing the steps required to produce the output and documenting the policies, procedures, and work instructions currently in use. This information is indispensable for helping PMT members reach a common understanding of the current process and, in the design phase, it simplifies the task of revamping the existing process or designing a new process since it helps the designers avoid earlier problems.

An as-is diagram provides process visibility and promotes process understanding.

The process map consists of two essential elements: (1) a diagram of the process steps, often referred to as the as-is diagram; and (2) a collection of related information about the process, its documentation. Taken together, these elements are particularly useful for determining the scope of the change required to complete the next two phases of the project: design and implementation.

---

*Louis J. De Rose in his book *The Value Network* defines value as, "the satisfaction of customer requirements at the least cost of acquisition, ownership and use."

The as-is diagram can be prepared in one of two ways: First, the PMT can begin with a preliminary diagram prepared by the PMT leader before the group session. Basically, it would reflect the leader's personal experience and knowledge of the process. It could then be confirmed by other people who know the process, but are not members of the PMT. Finally, the PMT would review and update the diagram in a one-day group session.

The second, and preferred, method is to have the PMT leader or a facilitator conduct a one- or two-day brainstorming session. The diagram would be developed from scratch based on the PMT members' knowledge and experience with the process. A common way of capturing the process steps is to use Post-it™ notes on brown paper as team members throw them out for discussion. Later, the individual notes can be arranged or rearranged into the proper sequence and annotated with flow arrows and text notes.

Later, the information collected should be formalized electronically and distributed to PMT members. To help the PMT recorder (a member of the team who is responsible for recording and organizing process information) organize the steps of the as-is diagram, a technique referred to as *abstraction* is often used. An abstraction occurs when a group of steps from a lower-level diagram are summarized into a single step on a higher-level diagram, as shown in Figure 5.4.

A lower-level diagram will generally contain the very basic process steps, such as gathers, selects, calculates, or queues operations. These steps can then be abstracted into a higher-level action such as prepares. In a well-executed diagram, a majority of the steps on the higher-level diagram have been abstracted from lower-level steps.

A conceptual walkthrough promotes common understanding and ensures that the process picture is complete.

After the diagram has been constructed and the individual members have reviewed the output, the PMT leader conducts a *conceptual walkthrough* to make sure that the diagram is as complete a picture of the process as possible. The conceptual walkthrough is critical because the as-is diagram is the backdrop for documenting and analyzing the process. Thus, it is crucial that it be as accurate as possible.

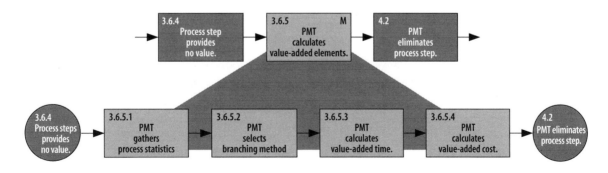

Figure 5.4: **Abstracting process steps.**

One of the most important reasons for creating an as-is diagram is to ensure that existing problems are not duplicated in the redesigned process. It is also beneficial for measuring the value of a proposed process innovation.

Additionally, if the simple sentence structure* technique (described in an earlier section) is used in the diagram, a precise picture of the process will be produced. Thus, PMT members will achieve a greater understanding and appreciation of the entire process.

Step 3.4   Process Team Prepares Process Documentation

The as-is diagram represents only a small portion of the information the process map should incorporate. The diagram's purpose is to graphically show the flow of work or information so that the PMT members have a clear understanding of the complete process flow. A thoroughly described process, however, requires a much more comprehensive set of documentation.

It is important to collect performance data to get some indication of how effectively the process operates.

Therefore, the fourth step is to gather both descriptive and statistical information about each step shown on the as-is diagram—and for the process in its entirety. Information, such as how the process is controlled and its support mechanisms, needs to be identified, collected, and recorded. It is also important to collect performance data to give some indication of how effectively the process operates and how efficiently internal processes are producing the required output.

Documenting the process is shown as a separate step in the process analysis, but the information is really collected throughout the entire process. Probably the best way to capture the data initially is with easel paper and Post-it™ notes during a group diagramming session.

The data collected should be analyzed and summarized into a formal document during this step. That is, this step can be dedicated to reviewing, analyzing, summarizing, and formalizing the presentation of all of the process information.

Step 3.5   Process Team Verifies As-Is Process Map

In step 5, the PMT uses the process map to conduct a physical walkthrough. This is accomplished by observing the people who actually perform the work and noting any differences encountered in the diagram and documentation. The walkthrough helps the PMT members ensure that the as-is dia-

---

*Based on concepts presented by Noam Chomsky, *Language and Problems of Knowledge: The Managua Lectures* (Cambridge, Mass.: MIT Press, 1988).

gram and related documentation accurately describe the entire process and that all of the members have the same level of understanding of the process.

Three useful suggestions for conducting an effective walkthrough are as follows:

A physical walkthrough is invaluable for noting differences in the way people perform their work.

1. Follow the most logical unit of work as it actually flows through the process. The most logical unit may be a discrete item or batch, or it may relate to a specific service, such as processing an engineering change notice.

2. When following a batch, be aware that the batch size may change from work area to work area, and that the batch size for movement may be different than the batch size worked on.

3. PMT members should ask the people doing the work to describe what they do in their own words. Then compare this description to the documentation collected by other means. Differences should be explored to determine which source needs to be corrected.

It is also important to note any variations in the way different people perform the same steps in the process, especially where more than one person is doing the same job. In fact, a walkthrough is invaluable for noting these differences, especially since this information is difficult to obtain any other way.

Step 3.6 Process Team Performs Value-Added Assessment

The final step in the process analysis phase is to conduct a value-added assessment. To be able to complete this step, the information collected, summarized, and formalized in the previous five steps must be comprehensive enough to answer the following questions.

- What are the stakeholder's requirements?
- How well does the process meet the stakeholder's needs?
- What portion of the process adds value to the stakeholder?
- What are the inputs and outputs of each step in the process?
- What policies, procedures, and work instructions inhibit the smooth execution of the process?
- What issues prevent the effective and efficient execution of the process?
- How long does the process take? What is the process cycle time?
- What is the cost of the process?
- What information systems are used to support the process?

This final step in the process analysis phase is described in much greater detail in the next section.

Why Is a VAA Important?

VAA helps ensure that the stakeholder's requirements are met in the most effective way possible.

All processes transform inputs to produce an output: a physical product, information, report, or service for a stakeholder. In essence, the stakeholder describes what is of value to him or her about the output of the process; management defines the processes and structure required to support those needs; and employees perform the work to produce it. The objective of a VAA in relationship to this process is threefold.

First, to make sure the stakeholder's requirements are met in the most effective way possible. Ensuring that a process provides value to its stakeholders is the overriding determinant for including each step in the conversion process.

The stakeholder who receives a benefit from a process is the only one who can really define its value. This is true no matter who the stakeholder happens to be. The process established by management and followed by employees should always be based on these needs. Often, however, someone in the organization overdesigns a process owing to a lack a clear understanding of the requirements.

For example, "corporate or headquarters"—the operations in a large organization—typically requires its divisions and subsidiaries to abide by certain policies and procedures. These are requirements that are established to provide harmony among business processes.

VAA helps validate the structure management has put in place to manage its operations.

Meeting corporate management's requirements generally necessitates clarification by someone in the division or subsidiary. If it is done properly the process will provide the corporate headquarters with the output it needs to conduct its own business. If the requirements are interpreted improperly, however, then additional non–value-added steps will most likely enter the process design—even though managers may receive the information they need.

The second reason a VAA is important is that it will help to validate that the structure management has implemented actually supports the goal of meeting the stakeholder's requirements. This is often a difficult issue to address because management's interests are diverse and complex. It is an issue, however, that the PMT leader must fully research and candidly report.

VAA helps determine whether the people performing the work understand their assignments.

Third, a VAA is used to determine whether or not the people performing the work understand their assignments and are executing them as designed. Often a PMT will reach an erroneous conclusion about the flow of work because it is actually being done differently than devised by management. Redesigning a process based on wrong or misguided assumptions can waste everyone's time, and it can cost the company a significant amount of money.

Chapter 6

Framework for Analysis

Classifying Actions

A useful technique for abstracting classes of actions is shown in Table 6.1. It is intended to promote understanding of the non–value-added concept so that analyzing process steps is productive and efficient.

Both value-added and non–value-added actions can be categorized into one of the four phases of a typical process life cycle: plan, execute, review, and adapt.* The importance of classifying actions into one or more of the matrix cells shown is completely explained in the following sections.

Plan–VA

Planning

A planning step is one that prepares a detailed method, which is formulated prior to execution, for doing or making something. The detailed method

---

*Plan, execute, review, and adapt are used in higher levels of a process diagram to highlight the scope of work being defined and documented. The traditional plan, do, check, act paradigm of quality programs is much narrower in scope, and, therefore, more useful at the task level.

Table 6.1: Plan, execute, review, adapt cycle.

Phase	Abstraction	
	Value-added actions (VA)	**Non–value-added actions (NVA)**
Plan	Planning	Preparation
Execute	Execution	Storage, movement, and handling
Review	Prevention	Control
Adapt		Processing defects and waste

describes a plan, scheme, program, project, or outline that is used to take the steps necessary to complete a particular activity.

Planning is a value-added step because the results will generally be superior.

Planning is a value-added step because the results achieved will generally be better, proceed with greater speed, and be more adaptable to change than would be the case if no plan was in place. Of course, one of the goals of planning is to reduce the chance of error and minimize rework. The value of planning is to reduce errors, lower cost, and produce the output quickly.

Traditionally, planning has been viewed as a predominantly managerial function that was broadly applied to the entire business, not to detailed tasks. More detailed kinds of tasks, however, also require planning. For example, the person who prepares a detailed set of instructions, such as how to schedule equipment or design a new product, is also engaged in planning.

Planning lower-level activities is just as important as developing the higher-level business planning.

Of course, planning lower-level activities is just as important as the higher-level business planning. For example, an engineer who prepares a prototype of a product to validate its design is engaged in planning. The prototype may provide an opportunity to work out production problems before they actually occur. Without such a prototype, it is likely that significant changes in the production process would be required along the way.

The same consequence is also possible at abstract levels of planning. For example, if a strategic plan is prepared but never communicated throughout the organization, the entire process may be of no value to anyone. The potency of all planning efforts needs to be periodically assessed to ensure that they do, in fact, contribute value to the intended stakeholder; that is, management.

Table 6.2: Non–value-added preparation actions.

	Action	Synonyms	Related actions	Diagramming symbol
Preparation	**Assigns**	Allocates Appoints	Consigns Designates Distributes	work
	Requests	*None*	*None*	work
	Sets up	Establishes	Arranges Organizes Prepares	work
	Stages	Stores	Schedules	work

Plan–NVA

Preparation

A process step in which someone makes an object ready or suitable for a specific purpose is a preparation step. Alternately, if the process step provides, equips, or furnishes someone with the necessary information, items, provisions, or accessories to perform a subsequent step, it is also a preparation step.

Table 6.2 lists four actions—with synonyms and related actions—that generally fall into the preparation category. As a general rule, a preparation step executes in anticipation of performing a subsequent step. For example, if a computer operator needs to request a particular file before being able to process it further, the act of requesting the file is a preparation step for the subsequent processing step. Such steps typically add no value to the stakeholder of the process.

In a manufacturing environment, setting up a machine to produce a component part is generally a fertile area for locating wasted time and resources. Setting up a machine has become so ingrained in the company's standard operating procedure that management is often reluctant to even discuss the possibility of improving the process.

When studying a setup procedure, the goal is not necessarily to eliminate the setup step completely, but to reduce the time required to the lowest value possible. Companies have achieved remarkable results—sometimes by a factor of 10—in reducing cycle time in this particular step of a process.

Execute–VA

Execution

By definition, every process step converts some kind of input into output. That is, each step acts on an object, or executes to produce an output. If the process is well designed, it will produce the output in the shortest possible time, with the highest quality possible.

Therefore, to determine whether or not a step adds value, execution refers to the transformation of information, the output of a product, or the delivery of a service that directly meets a stakeholder's needs. To add value, a process step must meet two key requirements: First, the output must be something that provides value to the stakeholder; and second, completing the step is actually necessary to provide the required output.

In very large organizations, ensuring that these two requirements are actually met becomes a real challenge because interference from the functional organizations—teams that were originally created to facilitate activities—gets in the way. People's attention is often focused on achieving functional results rather than meeting stakeholders' needs.

In many organizations, the farther away the person providing the service is from the stakeholder, the greater the likelihood that non–value-added work will creep into the process. Therefore, execution processes must be constantly reviewed to ensure that all of the steps are truly needed and that the work can adapt quickly to changes in stakeholders' needs.

To add value, a process step must provide value to the stakeholder and be necessary to the output.

Execute–NVA

Storage

A process step that places a product, information, or service in a holding area (file, inventory location, or refrigerator) or position (queue) for use or service at a later time is considered a storage action. Refer to Table 6.3 for a list of actions in the storage category.

For example, when people wait in line for service at a grocery store, they are waiting in a queue. For diagramming purposes this can be described as "Customers wait for grocery checkout." In this case the procedure places customers in a queue until the "Checkout clerk records [the] customers' purchases."

This is a rather simple example, but the fact is that customers must wait in a line until one of the grocery store's checkout clerks can record the customers' purchases. One of the reasons for inconveniencing customers in such a manner is to properly maintain the store's inventory records. Even through this procedure is of little immediate concern to customers, the

Table 6.3: Non–value-added storage actions.

	Action	Synonyms	Related actions	Diagramming symbol
Storage	**Files**	Catalogs Classifies	Deposits Records	store
	Records	Documents	Enters Files Inputs Labels Posts Transcribes	work
	Updates	Edits	Recreates Restores	work
	Waits for	Delays Pauses	Halts Stops	delay

long-term health of the store may be dependent on accurate inventory records.

The customers' immediate goal, of course, is to spend as little time as possible in the queue. Therefore, anything that the store owner can do to meet the customers' need, without interfering with the need to keep accurate inventory records, would probably result in increased business for the store.

Execute–NVA

Movement and Handling

A process step that causes someone or something to change the place or position of an object, whether it is information or a physical product, is classified as a movement or handling action. Table 6.4 provides a list of commonly used actions in this category.

The challenge is to find a way to reduce both the time and cost of moving and handling activities.

Compelling someone to move an object any distance rarely adds value to the stakeholder. Movement and handling actions generally take time that could probably be eliminated if the process were designed differently. The challenge is to find creative ways to accomplish the same thing without adding time and cost.

Table 6.4: Non–value-added movement and handling actions.

	Action	Synonyms	Related actions	Diagramming symbol
Movement and handling	**Collates**	Sorts Separates	Compares Organizes	work
	Collects	Accumulates Gathers	Assembles Compiles	work
	Copies	Duplicates Reproduces	Transcribes	work
	Delivers	Distributes Submits Transfers	Issues	work
	Distributes	Issues	Faxes Mails Sends	work
	Issues	Distributes	Delivers Pushes	work
	Loads	Fills	Accumulates Stacks	work
	Moves	Carries Pulls Pushes	Retrieves Sends Transmits	work
	Receives	Admits	Accepts Acquires Obtains Takes	work

Of course, movement and handling actions are needed to accomplish many tasks, such as when transporting finished goods to customers. Therefore, in assessing a process for value-added, the challenge is to find a way to reduce both the time and cost of moving the product. For example, instead of shipping product 3000 miles by truck, perhaps it would be cheaper and faster to build a plant near the market being served.

Excessive movement and handling can be minimized or eliminated by rearranging equipment in a manufacturing plant or by changing the flow of paperwork through the various departments in an office.

Often movement and handling issues must be balanced with inventory storage issues. That is, if a goal to reduce storage is established, then how the product is moved becomes much more important, since storage queues would be significantly reduced in favor of just-in-time procedures. This illustrates the point that doing one thing without due consideration for the other could have unfortunate results.

Review—VA

Prevention

Steps specifically designed to prevent poor quality in products or services fall into the prevention category. If properly designed, these steps will not only prevent process defects in succeeding steps, but will also eliminate or minimize the need to establish unnecessary control steps during the process.

Establishing preventive processes is an essential tool management uses to ensure a smooth-running business.

Process steps performed to avoid future occurrences of a problem can also be considered prevention actions. For example, measuring and analyzing steps established to determine when a process is outside of tolerance limits is a preventive step. That is, if the steps were not in place, the quality of the product or service would suffer without a clue as to what is causing the problem.

Establishing preventive processes is a fundamental tool management uses to ensure a smooth-running process—one that is efficient, flexible, and effective. Of course, caution must be exercised to ensure that the steps put in place are actually necessary. Of equal importance is eliminating controls when the corrective measures have restored the process to its preproblem state.

For example, if a heavily used scale has not been calibrated for a long period of time, it may provide inaccurate readings. Calibrating the scale after it is found to be inaccurate will certainly correct the problem. But relying on finding the problem after it occurs ignores the error in the process; that is, defects will continue to occur. If the process is changed to prevent the scale from becoming inaccurate in the first place, the problem would probably go away completely.

Review—NVA

Process Control

Process control steps are associated with measuring, evaluating, or auditing information, products, or services to assure conformance to specifications and performance requirements. A control step acts on the output of a prior process step for the purpose of identifying and reporting defects from the process after they have occurred. Table 6.5 provides a list of commonly used actions in the process control category.

Table 6.5: Non–value-added control actions.

	Action	Synonyms	Related actions	Diagramming symbol
Process control	**Approves**	Certifies Endorses Ratifies	Recommends	work
	Expedites	Facilitates	Coordinates Dispatches	work
	Identifies	Classifies	Analyzes Describes	inspect
	Inspects	Audits Checks Tests Verifies	Examines Investigates Searches for	inspect
	Labels	Marks Tags	Records	work
	Measures	Counts Weighs	Calibrates	work
	Monitors	Observes Regulates Supervises	Controls	inspect
	Reviews	Audits Analyzes Examines Inspects	Checks Investigates Tests Verifies	inspect
	Selects	Chooses	*None*	work
	Verifies	Confirms Documents Validates	Establishes Ratifies Reconciles Supports Tests	work

A control technique that has been abused over the years is management approvals. When a process take a long time to complete, and the cost of the output is high, it is common to control the situation with reviews and approvals that simply take too long.

By the time the process reaches the execution phase, a considerable amount of time and cost have already been accumulated with very little output to show for it. And in most cases, instituting additional reviews and approvals almost never helps a project manager achieve success. While such actions as reviews, approvals, inspections, and decisions are necessary to control and adapt processes as conditions change, they should be used sparingly and as early in the process as possible.

Adapt–NVA

Processing Defects

A step created to process defects—in information, products, or services—often adds no value to the overall process. Generally, defects are the result of an output not conforming to performance standards, processing requirements, or stakeholder needs. Table 6.6 provides a list of commonly used actions in the processing defects category.

Defects are generally due to an internal or external failure of some kind. Internal failures occur prior to the delivery or shipment of the product or the furnishing of a service.

Table 6.6: Non–value-added processing defects actions.

	Action	Synonyms	Related actions	Diagramming symbol
Processing defects	**Adjusts**	Adapts	Accommodates Conforms to	work
	Changes	Adjusts Aters Modifies Corrects	Converts Conforms to Edits Revises	work
	Maintains	Cleans Repairs	Fixes	work
	Reconciles	None	Adapts Adjusts Determines	work
	Repairs	Fixes Reworks	Changes Maintains Revises	work
	Returns	Restores Refunds	Replaces	work
	Revises	Corrects Edits Reworks	Adjusts Alters Changes	work

Table 6.7: Non–value-added processing waste actions.

	Action	Synonyms	Related actions	Diagramming symbol
Processing waste	**Eliminates**	Removes	Cancels Disposes of	work

Defects are generally due to an internal or external failure of some kind.

The time and cost lost due to internal failures is often hidden from the stakeholder since it occurs within the control of management. Nevertheless, the stakeholder pays for internal failures through the price of the product or service.

External failures occur during or after the delivery of the product or service to the stakeholder. Although product failures are often covered by a warranty or guarantee, they really add no value to the stakeholder. And service failures almost always cause the loss of future business to the service provider.

A root cause analysis* (RCA) of internal and external failures should always be conducted to determine how the process could be redesigned to minimize them. One way of accomplishing this is to perform a failure analysis with the goal of preventing future defects. Instituting an RCA process can be considered a preventive, that is, value-added, step because it does enhance the overall process by eliminating the need to rework or repair unsuitable outputs.

Adapt–NVA

Processing Waste

A step required to process scrap or waste is a non–value-added step. Scrap refers to processing defects that cannot be reworked or redone. On the other hand, waste is a by-product of a step, and waste must be discarded or recycled. The activity of eliminating or removing waste is a non–value-added activity. Table 6.7 provides a list of commonly used actions in the processing waste category.

If material from a trimming operation in a plastics plant gets contaminated because of poor work center cleaning procedures, it must be scrapped. If, however, the work procedures were modified to ensure that the material remained clean, it could be reprocessed and used again. In both instances, the process adds both time and cost to the end product and needs to be managed. The obvious objective in studying the cause of waste is to find a way to ensure that it is not generated in the first place.

---

*Root cause analysis or problem solving involves the following: defining the problem and its symptoms; formulating theories (through cause-and-effect diagrams); testing the theories (data collection); and identifying root causes (analysis of the collected data) for the problem. The purpose of this analysis is to find the underlying or "root" cause as manifested by the symptoms.

CHAPTER 7

Value-Added Assessment Process

The Assessment Process

Figure 7.1 shows a seven-step procedure for sorting out value-added and non–value-added activities in a process. It has two parallel paths that direct the PMT's decision to one state or the other based on the type of stakeholder group being served: customer or noncustomer.

Before the PMT can begin its assessment, it needs input from two other business processes, both of which are external to the process analysis effort. First the PMT needs to know what management's objectives for the business are; this is shown as step 1.1. Second, the PMT needs to know who the stakeholders of the process are; this is shown as step 2.2. It is assumed that this input was developed as a part of the organization's strategy management and process management processes. If this information is not available to the PMT, it is doubtful that the sorting-out process will be effective and the result could be of questionable value.

Step 1.1 Management Establishes Business Objectives

The strategy management process (SMP), which unquestionably has business value, is senior management's customary way of establishing and communicating its vision, goals, and objectives for the business to all of its stakeholder groups.

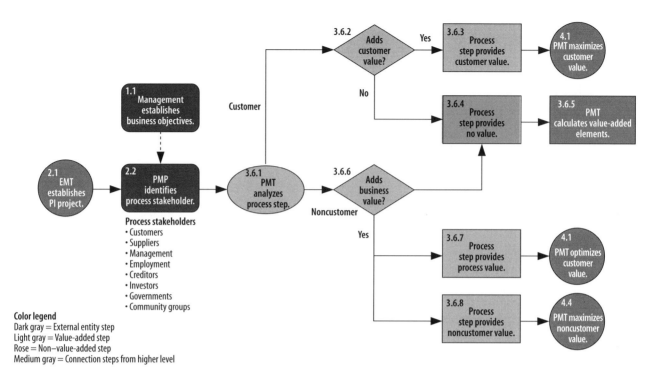

Figure 7.1. Value-added assessment process.

Management's responsibility is to make sure that every objective meets the principle of satisfying a stakeholder's need.

The vision is a broad statement of where the leaders of the organization want it to go. A vision statement is generally valuable to all stakeholders because it provides them with clues of how people will conduct themselves in business dealings. Its value, however, is related more to a feeling of goodness rather than to a direct effect on the business relationship between any of the groups.

Business goals are slightly narrower and more focused assertions about what management believes it needs to accomplish in the long run. These beliefs are sometimes tied to the needs of the stakeholders—particularly customers—but not necessarily in a direct way. For most companies, goals are simply internal targets.

Objectives are specific and concrete statements, which denote both time and outcome statistics, that provide management with a short-term target for accomplishing what it believes the stakeholders want. If the objectives are developed in cooperation with the stakeholders, it is likely that their needs will be met. If not, time and money will be wasted in the attempt to achieve them.

Ultimately, the effectiveness of a process is determined by the principle of satisfying stakeholders' needs. To achieve this end, management's responsibility is to make sure that every objective it establishes also meets this principle. Therefore, it is important that the relationship between management's objectives and stakeholders' needs be completely understood before the PMT begins the VAA process.

Step 2.2   PMP Identifies Process Stakeholder

Like the previous step, the process management process (PMP) step of identifying process stakeholders is usually performed outside of the scope of the process analysis phase of the improvement project. That is, the stakeholders are identified during the PMP process and provided as input into this step.*

The PMT will then review the information to gain a thorough understanding of how each stakeholder group interfaces with the process being studied. If the information is incomplete or not available, then the PMT will have to develop it using chapter 1, "Business Stakeholders" (see pp. 5–15), as a guide.

What to Look For

PMT members often disagree and become hostile about other members' views and classifications.

The task of sorting out non–value-added activities is never as simple and clear-cut as it may appear to be. In fact, PMT members often aggressively disagree and become hostile about other members' views and classifications.

Often the dispute will develop around a regulatory control step, such as approvals, or where counting, moving, or sorting the product is involved. The following examples show how this controversy may begin when reviewing these kinds of actions.

- *Approvals*   One signature on a document may be value-added for the organization, but other signatures may not be.
- *Counting*   Counting something once might be value-added, but additional counts to verify the same items are generally not.
- *Moving and storing*   Storing material in a freezer for conditioning may be value-added, but other moving and storage actions may not be.

Assessing whether or not a particular task adds value is not a science—and there is no magic to the analysis.

- *Sorting*   Sorting documents into categories to assign work to individual participants might be value-added if a particular skill is required, but multiple sorts of the same documents may not be.
- *Inspecting*   Often considered a good practice for controlling quality, inspecting something is another activity that provokes a considerable amount of discussion during the analysis process.

It does not seem to matter what process is being analyzed, certain actions or verbs consistently emerge as being potentially non–value-added.

---

*The process management organization is the function that is responsible for managing process improvement projects. This may be human resources, finance, engineering, or a reengineering group specifically created for this purpose.

Therefore, when mapping processes, it is beneficial for an analyst to maintain a list of potentially non–value-added actions, such as the list provided in the dictionary section of this book (see pp. 115–118).

It must be clearly understood, however, that assessing whether or not a particular task adds value is not a science—and there is no magic to the framework discussed. Nevertheless, it is important to follow such a framework to keep the PMT focused on the stakeholders' needs—rather than on its own interests. Furthermore, this focus will significantly improve the quality of the process analysis.

Question Beliefs and Assumptions

As the PMT progresses through the VAA process, it is important that each member challenge the beliefs and assumptions behind each step to determine the rationale for including it in the process. When questioning a particular step, some managers may—based on their knowledge of how things work—regard it as value-added, but after further study, it may not be.

Question everyone's beliefs and assumptions about how things really work.

For example, an engineering department may routinely create a detailed design drawing that it believes is valuable to workers on the shop floor. After speaking with the workers, however, the PMT may find that workers really have no need for the drawing because they work from the product's dimensions. Components remain the same, but the dimensions change—no matter how the design is changed. In this case, distributing the design drawings is definitely a non–value-added step that should be eliminated.

Step 3.6.1 PMT Analyzes Process Step

This is the first step in the sorting-out process where the PMT will sort the process steps into one of two stakeholder piles for further analysis: customer and noncustomer.

If no stakeholder surfaces, the process step should be targeted for elimination.

To complete this task, the PMT must review and become familiar with management's business objectives and each stakeholder group's requirements. Then the PMT will be prepared to analyze each step individually to determine which stakeholder group receives the greatest benefit, or has the greatest influence on the execution of the step. At this point, the PMT is examining each step to determine on which parallel path to send the step for further analysis: customer value or business value.

If the process does not appear to have a stakeholder, its context should be expanded to determine if it is part of a higher-level process that does contribute value to a stakeholder. If no stakeholder surfaces at this point, the process step should be targeted for elimination because it probably adds no real value to the business.

Step 3.6.2   Process Step Adds Customer Value?

This is a decision step. If it has been determined that the process step adds value to the customer, the information will be passed along to the next step, number 3.6.3—process step provides customer value. Otherwise, the step will be passed to step 3.6.4—process step provides no value.

Step 3.6.3   Process Step Provides Customer Value

The difficulty in determining whether or not a process has customer value originates when examining individual tasks.

The purpose of step 3.6.3 is to clarify the nature of customer value and begin exploring ways to maximize value. Processes that reach this step add *real* value and are *essential* to meeting customers' requirements; that is, the external customer who purchases the company's products or services.

Management's objective is to maximize the efficiency and flexibility of these processes on the customers' behalf. In this context, a value-added step is one that has one or more of the following characteristics.

- Physically changes the work passing through it
- Is requested by the customer
- Is legally required or mandated by the customer
- Is something the customer is willing to pay for

The difficulty in determining whether or not a process has customer value originates when examining individual tasks. For example, the regulatory requirements in most industries do not specify step-by-step activities for compliance, but they do specify what the required outcome should be.

Therefore, the actual steps required to arrive at the outcome have probably been dictated by an internal function in the organization—quality control, regulatory affairs, or finance—often under the assumption of being required by the regulatory agency. If the required outcome can be achieved by excluding one of the steps specified, then that step is not adding value and could be eliminated permanently.

The objective in analyzing related processes is to find ways of maximizing the value added to the customer. In fact, many companies believe that exceeding customers' needs is an excellent goal to pursue. Judicious use of technology is usually the preferred means for achieving this goal.

Step 3.6.6   Process Step Adds Business Value?

This is a decision step. If it has been determined that the process step adds value to the business, the information will be passed along to one of the next two steps, number 3.6.7—process step provides process value, or number 3.6.8—process step provides noncustomer value. Otherwise, control will pass to step 3.6.4—process step provides no value.

Process steps that add business value are activities performed to meet the needs of running a viable business. Included in this category would be activities necessary to meet policy, accounting, employee, shareholder, and regulatory requirements.

Process steps that add business value are activities performed to meet the needs of running a viable business.

As a general rule, business processes are created by management to meet the needs of noncustomer groups such as suppliers, management, employees, creditors, investors, governments, or community groups. The noncustomer processes are conceived in an effort to satisfy one of these groups, and permit the business to prosper so that it can continue to provide products and services to its customers.

Without a doubt, these noncustomer activities add cost to the product or service delivered to the customer and are often perceived, from a customer's perspective, as being non–value-added. It could be argued, however, that they add customer value indirectly because without many of them (for example, paying taxes) the company would not be able to continue operations.

In some cases, customers may be willing to pay for regulatory requirements since customers cannot use the product unless it is in compliance with regulations. This is particularly true in health- or environment-related businesses such as pharmaceuticals, medical services, and nuclear energy.

Step 3.6.7   Process Step Provides Process Value

Management often establishes processes to help in monitoring or controlling the physical production process. If these monitor-and-control processes truly provide management with the information it needs, they are considered value-added. If, on the other hand, the controls and reviews are simply in place to provide substance to a management position, then they have no real value and should be eliminated.

The downsizing of middle management positions over the past five years has been, for the most part, the elimination of these kinds of nonvalue activities. Positions that were established to provide upper management with a degree of confidence that resources were being well managed were eliminated primarily through better use of computer technology.

Process value refers to the activities established to help managers execute the planning and prevention areas of their jobs.

Process value refers to the activites established to help managers execute the planning and prevention areas of their jobs.

- *Planning* is the detailed method, formulated prior to execution, for doing or making something. The detailed method describes a plan, scheme, program, or project; that is, the set of steps necessary to complete a task.

- *Prevention* steps help avoid poor quality in products or services. These steps prevent processing defects in succeeding steps, often eliminating or minimizing the need for control steps. Steps implemented to prevent the future occurrence of a problem are considered prevention steps.

While planning and prevention activities do not directly add customer value, they do establish the environment for creating value by providing the resources, structure, and communications necessary to ensure that customers' needs are met. If these activities are done properly, an efficient and flexible process will accomplish the desired end.

On the other hand, management, administrative, and control functions typically do not add value.

The objective in analyzing steps for process value is to optimize the efficiency of the processes established by management for its own purposes.

- *Control* steps are associated with measuring, evaluating, or auditing information, products, or services to ensure conformance to specifications and performance requirements.

- Additionally, control steps act on the output of a prior process step and identify processing defects after they have occurred. While these steps catch problems with the product or service, they do not enhance either the product or service, nor do they contribute to improving the process.

- Most *administrative* activities relate to or support control steps. Therefore, they do not add value to the process.

The objective in analyzing steps for process value is to optimize the efficiency of the processes established by management for its own purposes. Here again, technology is a useful tool for accomplishing this goal.

Step 3.6.8   Process Step Provides Noncustomer Value

There are a number of processes in an organization that are critical to running the business but that do not appear to meet the requirements of adding value for which the customer is willing to pay. The PMT might question whether the process is of value to a stakeholder or if it should be eliminated.

An action step that normally adds value may become a non–value-added step—or vice versa—in a particular circumstance. For example, suppose an administrative assistant types a supply requisition. Normally this is considered a value-added step in the process of creating a purchase order.

After further study, however, it is discovered that the administrative assistant receives a handwritten requisition from a professional employee before sending it to a data entry operator who types it into the purchasing system. In this case, the administrative assistant typing a supply requisition is a non–value-added step. Once again, the goal in analyzing processes that add value is to maximize the value added to the recipient of the output.

Step 3.6.4 Process Step Provides No Value

Non–value-added activities exist because the process is inadequately designed or the process is not functioning as designed.

If the PMT's analysis reaches this point, the process step probably does not add value to any of the stakeholder groups. Management should work to eliminate the activities in this step.

Non–value-added activities do not contribute to satisfying customer or other stakeholder requirements. These activities exist because the process is inadequately designed or it is not functioning as designed.

- When the process is inadequately designed, there are steps in the process required for preparation, storage, movement, and waste disposal.
- When the process does not function as designed, the process contains steps to control (monitor, evaluate, or measure) and manage defects in the product or service such as rework and scrap.*

A step is considered non–value-added if it meets any of the following criteria.

- If the stakeholder is a customer, a non–value-added step is one for which the customer is unwilling to pay, and one that does not change the work output in a way that makes it more valuable to the customer.
- A non–value-added step does not contribute positively to the requirements of one or more of the other stakeholders.
- The process step does not contribute to the effectiveness, efficiency, or flexibility of the process. Often the action directly indicates a non–value-added step. Examples include activities such as review, approve, rework, move, store, and file.

The goal here is to eliminate these steps entirely. Since they do not contribute any value to the stakeholders of the process, they can be eliminated without affecting the product or service.

---

*The NVA dictionary (see chapter 9) explains why *preparation, storage,* and so on are examples of *inadequate* design.

Concluding Thoughts

First, throughout the entire analysis session, challenge all assumptions about the process—no matter who wants to clutch onto them. Remember, a step may appear to add value, but closer examination of the underlying assumptions often discloses that it is really not necessary, it could be eliminated without any impact to the delivery of the product or service.

Second, if a non–value-added step provides output that is necessary and essential for a subsequent step, then it follows that the succeeding steps are also non–value-added.

Third, a parent step—one that contains one or more lower-level steps— is value-added if at least one step in the lower-level diagram is value-added—even though every other step in the diagram is determined to be non–value-added. If all of the steps at the child level are non–value-added, then it follows that the parent step is also non–value-added.

Fourth, communicating information often involves some form of conversion in either media or content. Analyzing an information processing step to determine if it adds value follows the same logic as a step that transforms material or services.

• Thus, preparing a statistical process control chart (prevention), preparing a master schedule (planning), and providing directions to a destination (conversion) are typically value-added steps.

• Preparing a budget variance report (control), reprocessing an insurance claim (processing a defect), entering or recording a customer order (storage), distributing a product overstock memo (movement and handling), and searching for a customer's file (preparation) are examples of non–value-added information processing steps.

Finally, communication is the act of providing information through some form or medium. Communications are neither value-added nor non–value-added. It is the *purpose* of the communication that determines whether or not the step is value-added or non–value-added.

Chapter 8

Process Time and Cost Elements

The final step in a VAA is to calculate value-added time and cost elements for the process. These calculations provide the PMT with the value-added content of the process and the critical path, and establish the benchmark values used in the process design phase of a project.

A VAA will often show that 60 percent to 70 percent of the time and cost in a given process can be eliminated without affecting its output. Therefore, the PMT's challenge is to identify and document this waste.

The steps taken by the PMT are shown in Figure 8.1. It is a four-step process for collecting the raw data, calculating the value-added statistics, and summarizing the information up the hierarchy to determine the total process time and cost.

The last two steps are shown with a loop back because the calculations are done at each level of the process hierarchy. For example, Figure 8.2 shows a lower-level process diagram that will be used to start the calculation of value-added time—step 3.6.5.3, and value-added cost—step 3.6.5.4.

Once these calculations have been completed, the PMT would use the values to update step 8 in the higher-level diagram shown in Figure 8.3. This is an abstraction of the lower-level diagram.

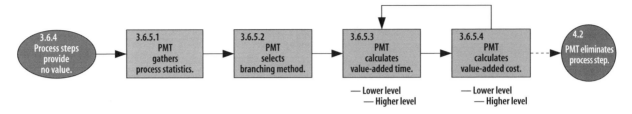

Figure 8.1:   PMT calculates value-added elements.

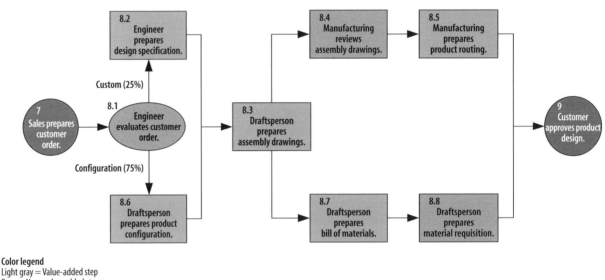

Engineering prepares product design.

Color legend
Light gray = Value-added step
Rose = Non–value-added step
Medium gray = Connection steps from higher level

Figure 8.2:   Low-level process diagram.

If there were more layers in the hierarchy, the calculation process would continue upward until the data have been summarized to the highest level of abstraction. Figures 8.2 and 8.3 will be used throughout this section to illustrate the principles and procedures for calculating process time and cost at all levels.

Once these values have been determined, it may be necessary to delve deeper into the statistics. For example, if a wide range of values are found in the data, it is important for the PMT to gain an understanding of the cause of this variability. But the work needed to analyze it should be addressed as a separate subject, outside the scope of the VAA.

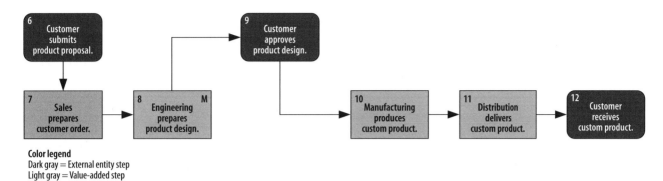

Figure 8.3: **High-level process diagram.**

Step 3.6.5.1 PMT Gathers Process Statistics

The first step is to gather process time and cost statistics for each individual process step. When gathering these statistics, it is important to collect them at the lowest level of the diagram first, and then summarize them up the hierarchy to the highest level.

Gather statistics at the lowest level of the diagram first.

The degree of statistical accuracy depends on the amount of time and number of people available for data collection. The following methods, shown in the order of decreasing accuracy, are appropriate for gathering raw data.

- Utilize existing data sources, such as accounting records or resource time sheets, which may be accessible in computer format or available from existing files.

- Develop an interim data collection form for recording time and cost data during the physical walkthrough of the process.

- Follow an item or group of items through the process, recording the data while observing the process.

- Ask the experts—the people doing the work—to provide an estimate.

The PMT can actually use any method it deems appropriate in the circumstances. The important thing to remember is that the data collected or estimated must be complete enough to calculate the statistics necessary to abstract the information for the entire diagram.

When gathering the information for the lowest possible level in the diagram, the PMT should keep the following data collection guidelines in mind.

Most work time is measured in minutes while most wait time is measured in hours or days. Consequently, work time is relatively small in comparison with total process time.

• The resource performing the work, whether a single person, machine, or a group, should be identified for each individual step.

• Identify a single time value for each step on the diagram; for example, work, setup, and wait.

• Wait time, idle time, or other delay steps should be clearly identified on the diagram.

When calculating the statistics at higher levels in the diagram, the PMT should keep the following guidelines in mind.

• At the very minimum, identify two time values, process and work time, for each step on the diagram.

• Process time, or cycle time, is the amount of elapsed time between the start of the step and its completion.

• The amount of time actually spent working on the output of a step is defined as work time.

• The difference between process time and work time is made up of other time factors, such as preparation steps or delays.

Resources represent a group of people, such as a team, department, or function, or machines. Therefore, to accurately calculate resource cost at all levels, the PMT should utilize the following rule: If the group performs the task collectively and equally, the labor or machine cost is the sum of the individual resource costs. If not, separate parallel steps or a lower-level process should be shown for each resource.

Input costs, such as raw materials, are only shown at the lowest levels in the process diagram. Generally, it is not necessary to include the cost of incidental inputs such as paper, pencils, oil, or disposable gloves, since they are generally included in the overhead rate calculation.

It is important to allocate overhead because it acts as a weighting factor to give emphasis to the cost differences between functions.

Overhead is the term generally used to describe miscellaneous process and nonprocess expenses that cannot be specifically identified to a particular step by usage. These costs are collected in accounts that are subsequently allocated to the products or services to calculate total costs. Often the accuracy of the calculated product cost depends on the method used to allocate overhead costs.

When analyzing processes, it is important to allocate overhead to process steps because it acts as a weighting factor to give emphasis to the impact of cost differences between functions. So much so, that results can be significantly influenced if the overhead rates are not applied.

The subject of allocating overhead is very complicated, however, and one that the PMT should not be engaged in during this particular analysis. In fact, it is recommended that the PMT use whatever method is employed for accounting purposes.

If the team feels that the results are being overly influenced by the assignment of overhead, a separate group should be formed to explore the issue. Frequently using a popular theory of cost allocated—direct costing, standard costs, or activity-based costing—provides greater accuracy.

Step 3.6.5.2 PMT Selects Branching Method

Selecting a branching method does not always apply to a process diagram. In fact, it is only performed in those cases where a process step branches into two or more alternate paths, as shown in Figure 8.2, step 8.3—a draftsperson prepares assembly drawings. Generally, this situation only occurs when a decision or inspection step permits the work flow to go down more than one path.

Averaging parallel paths is a quick way to determine aggregate cost for such tasks as scheduling and forecasting.

If a branch does occur, the PMT must determine which calculation of time and cost makes the most sense in the circumstances: Follow one of the alternate paths or calculate a weighted average of all of the possible paths.

For example, as shown in Figure 8.2, the customer has a choice of placing an order for a custom-designed product or purchasing a product configured from existing components. For illustration purposes, it is assumed that the company constantly sells configured products 75 percent of the time and custom-designed products 25 percent of the time.

Calculating alternate paths can provide valuable information about product or consumer groups.

Using the alternate path approach, the PMT would calculate the time and cost for both the configured and custom-designed products as shown in Table 8.1. If the PMT decides to take the custom-designed product path, the process time would be 12 hours—with three hours of work time—and the total cost would be $310.00. If the configured product path is chosen, the cost would be $175.00.

For a weighted average, the PMT would calculate the process time and cost by averaging the values for all of the possible paths using the probability, based on the sales mix, of taking the path as the weighting factor. For

Table 8.1: Alternate path time and cost.

Path	Probability factor	Process time	Work time	Process cost
Configuration	.75	7.0	2.0	$175.00
Custom design	.25	12.0	3.0	$310.00

Table 8.2: Calculating weighted time and cost.

Path	Probability factor	Process time	Weighted time	Process cost	Weighted cost
Configured	.75	7.0	5.25	$175.00	$131.25
Custom	.25	12.0	3.0	$310.00	77.50
	1.00		8.25		$208.75

example, in calculating the weighted average for the process shown in Figure 8.2, the following steps would be taken: First multiply the probability of taking a path by the time or cost for a path. This step is then repeated for all possible paths. Finally, the sum of these calculations returns the weighted average of all the paths as shown in Table 8.2. The weighted time and cost for custom-designed and configured products are 8.25 hours and $208.75, respectively.

Step 3.6.5.3 PMT Calculates Value-Added Time (Lower Level)

The calculation of process time starts at the lowest level in the hierarchy. As shown in Table 8.3, the process time, or the process cycle time, is calculated by adding the process times of all the individual steps. For this process, a step equals 62 hours. The steps with the strike-out line are not included in the totals.

The critical path is defined as the longest path through the process.

The next step is to determine the critical path. This is defined as the longest parallel path through the process—in terms of process time—from the first to the last step. A parallel path exists when a single process step triggers a branch to multiple process steps without any conditions; that is, the succeeding steps are performed at roughly the same time, and, therefore, occur in parallel.

When a parallel path exists, the PMT would determine which of the paths is the longest by adding up the process times for each path. For example, in step 8.3, engineering prepares product design diagram—a draftsperson prepares assembly drawings, triggering two separate, parallel paths. The first consists of Steps 8.4 and 8.5, and the other consists of steps 8.7 and 8.8.

Step 8.4—manufacturing reviews assembly drawings takes 10.0 hours to complete, and step 8.5—manufacturing prepares product routing takes 14.0 hours. This totals 24.0 hours.

On the other hand, step 8.7—draftsperson prepares bill of materials, takes 14.0 hours, and step 8.8—draftsperson prepares material requisition takes 11.0 hours for a total of 25.0 hours. Consequently, steps 8.7 and 8.8 are on the process critical path.

Table 8.3: PMT calculates value-added time (lower level).

Process step	Resource / action / resource	Process time (hours)	Work time (hours)	Value-added time
8.1	Engineer evaluates customer order.	15.0	3.0	
~~8.6~~	~~Draftsperson prepares product configuration.~~	~~7.0~~	~~2.0~~	
8.2	Engineer prepares design specification.	12.0	3.0	3.0
8.3	Draftsperson prepares assembly drawings.	10.0	2.0	2.0
~~8.4~~	~~Manufacturing reviews assembly drawings.~~	~~10.0~~	~~4.0~~	
~~8.5~~	~~Manufacturing prepares product routing.~~	~~14.0~~	~~5.0~~	
8.7	Draftsperson prepares bill of materials.	14.0	3.0	3.0
8.8	Draftsperson prepares material requisition.	11.0	3.0	
	Totals	62.0		8.0

Critical path (steps): 8.1, 8.2, 8.3, 8.7, 8.8   Percent value-added   12.9%

Therefore, the critical path for the engineering-prepares-product-design process consists of steps 8.1, 8.2 or 8.6, 8.3, 8.7, and 8.8. If the PMT chooses the custom-designed path when defining the alternate path, the critical path is 8.1, 8.6, 8.3, 8.7 and 8.8. But if the PMT used the weighted average approach, the critical path is 8.1, 8.2/8.6, 8.3, 8.7, and 8.8.

Finally, calculate the value-added time for the process. Following the critical path, add the work times of all of the value-added steps. Again, using the engineering-prepares-product-design process diagram, the value-added time is 8.0 hours, calculated from the work hours only, or 7.25 hours depending on the multiple branch method used. Also, remember that steps 8.1 and 8.5 are completely non–value-added.

To calculate the value-added percent, divide the value-added time by the total process time. In the example for the custom-designed product, the value-added hours are 8.0 divided by the total process time of 62.0 hours—multiplied by 100—equals a value-added of 12.9 percent.

Step 3.6.5.4   PMT Calculates Value-Added Cost (Lower Level)

Determining the process cost differs from calculating the process time for the following reason: Process time is the amount of time from the start of the process to its completion. When a process has parallel paths, only the longest path contributes to the total cycle time. The short paths do not impact the total cycle-time calculation.

Only the longest parallel path contributes to the total cycle time, but all paths affect the process cost.

In calculating process cost, however, parallel paths do impact the total cost of the process. Each path contributes a work component to the whole process and, thus, adds cost to the final process output. Therefore, to calculate process cost, the expense for every step on the diagram must be added, excluding, of course, step 8.6. This is shown in Table 8.4.

The calculation procedure is as follows: First calculate each individual process step and then accumulate them for the entire diagram. The final total will depend on the path taken in a multiple path diagram. In the engineering-prepares-product-design example, the total process cost is $2290.00 for the custom design path. The total cost using the weighted average approach—which is not shown in the table—is slightly less at $ 2189.00.

To calculate the value-added cost for the entire process, total the work times of all the value-added steps. Using the engineering-prepares-product-design diagram, the value-added cost is $1285.00 or $1184.00 depending on the branching method used. Remember that steps 8.1 and 8.5 are completely non–value-added.

Table 8.4: PMT calculates value-added cost (lower level).

Process step	Resource / action / resource	Labor costs	Input costs	Over-head costs	Process costs	Value-added costs
8.1	Engineer evaluates customer order.	$120.00	$ –	$200.00	$320.00	
~~8.6~~	~~Draftsperson prepares product configuration.~~	~~50.00~~	–	~~125.00~~	~~175.00~~	
8.2	Engineer prepares design specification.	120.00	–	190.00	310.00	$310.00
8.3	Draftsperson prepares assembly drawings.	50.00	–	120.00	170.00	170.00
8.4	Manufacturing reviews assembly drawings.	160.00	–	275.00	435.00	
8.5	Manufacturing prepares product routing.	200.00	100.00	300.00	600.00	600.00
8.7	Draftsperson prepares bill of materials.	75.00	–	130.00	205.00	205.00
8.8	Draftsperson prepares material requisition.	75.00	75.00	100.00	250.00	
	Totals	$800.00	$15.00	$1315.00	$2290.00	$1285.00

Critical path (steps): 8.1, 8.2, 8.3, 8.7, 8.8   Percent value-added   56.1%

The assumption is that all of the overhead is value-added because it makes the calculations easy. Since most accounting systems do not have the level of elegance necessary to break out overhead expenses by process steps, this is probably an acceptable alternative.

To calculate the percentage of value-added cost, divide the value-added cost by the total process cost. In this example, the percentage is calculated to be 56.1 percent. The percentage was calculated by dividing the value-added cost of $1285.00 by the total process cost of $ 2290.00. The percent value-added for the weighted average approach is 54.1 percent, or $1184.00 divided by $ 2189.00, multiplied by 100.

Step 3.6.5.3   PMT Calculates Value-Added Time (Higher Level)

After the lowest-level calculations are complete, the PMT can roll up the times to the next higher level in the diagram. As shown in Table 8.5, this is done by simply using the total process time and value-added time from the child process as the process time and value-added time for the parent process—step 8 in the product delivery process.

This procedure would continue for all of the process steps that have a lower-level diagram. Process steps without lower-level diagrams would use the same procedure outlined in steps 3.6.5.1 through 3.6.5.4.

Table 8.5: PMT calculates value-added time (higher level).

Process step	Resource / action / resource	Process time (hours)	Work time (hours)	Value-added time
6	Customer submits product proposal			
7	Sales prepares customer order	20.0	6.0	
8	Engineer prepares product design	62.0	14.0	8.0
9	Customer approves product design	40.0	0.0	
10	Manufacturing produces custom product	160.0	20.0	16.0
11	Distribution delivers customer product	24.0	2.0	2.0
12	Customer receives custom product			
	Totals	306.0	42.0	26.0
			Percent value-added	8.5%

Following the calculation of the process time at each level, steps 3.6.5.3 and 3.6.5.4 would be repeated at the next higher level until the entire process diagram is finished.

Step 3.6.5.4   PMT Calculates Value-Added Cost (Higher Level)

After the process costs have been calculated at the lowest levels, the PMT would roll up these costs to the next higher level in the diagram. As shown in Table 8.6, this is done by simply using the total process cost and value-added cost in the child process as the process cost and value-added cost for the parent process step, which is step 8 in the product delivery process.

This process would be continued for all of the process steps that have a lower-level process diagram. Process steps without lower-level diagrams would use the same procedure outlined in steps 3.6.5.1 through 3.6.5.4. Following the calculation of the process cost at each level, steps 3.6.5.3 and 3.6.5.4 would be repeated at the next higher level until the entire process diagram is finished.

Table 8.6:   PMT calculates value-added cost (higher level).

Process step	Resource / action / resource	Labor costs	Input costs	Over-head costs	Process costs	Value-added costs
6	Customer submits product proposal.					
7	Sales prepares customer order.	$180.00	$75.00	$250.00	$505.00	
8	Engineer prepares product design.	800.00	175.00	1315.00	2290.00	$1285.00
9	Customer approves product design.					
10	Manufacturing produces custom product.	400.00	1000.00	450.00	1850.00	975.00
11	Distribution delivers customer product.	40.00	50.00	100.00	190.00	190.00
12	Customer receives custom product.					
	Totals	$1420.00	$1300.00	$2115.00	$4835.00	$2450.00
					Percent value-added	50.7%

Paralysis Through Analysis

The scope of the VAA is intentionally narrow during this stage of the process analysis because the PMT is searching for clues as to which areas have the highest measure of inefficiency. Later, the PMT will focus its attention toward drilling down on the areas identified to determine root causes.

It is important for the PMT to keep its attention focused on identifying non–value-added activities.

The tendency, however, is to jump to conclusions about the nature of the inefficiencies and collect a significant amount of data that ultimately proves to be useless. Therefore, it is important that the PMT keep its efforts focused on identifying non–value-added activities and not spending too much time collecting and analyzing irrelevant data.* The following reminders will assist the team in this effort.

- **Data accuracy**   The accuracy of time and cost data is important, but not all that important during this phase. Whichever way gives the PMT a demonstrative picture of relative size and relationship will do the trick. In other words, don't get bogged down in a quagmire of data for the sake of accuracy.

- **Overhead allocations**   While it is important to determine the total cost of a process, it is not very productive to allocate overhead to a high degree of accuracy. Trying to determine precisely how to allocate overhead to each process is an art best left to functional experts outside the PMT.

It is easy to become inspired with the implied benefits of a new cost accounting paradigm like activity-based costing (ABC). The PMT should use whatever method its accounting department deems useful for the kind of analysis being done.

- **Process variability**   Process variability is also a very important statistic because it provides clues to potential problem areas. The amount of rigor used in arriving at these numbers should be limited to relatively simple calculations based on the collection of sample data. If, however, some of the process steps prove to be worth analyzing further, standard statistical and problem-solving techniques can be used.

- **Data collection bias**   The PMT leader should make sure that the methods and techniques developed to collect process data are as objective as possible. Project team members have often spent days, weeks, or months collecting data for the purpose of proving a point that, in the end, was not relevant to the process being studied. The PMT leader is the person who should prevent this situation by challenging the need for all data during the collection planning process.

---

*Michael Hammer and Steven A. Stanton, *The Reengineering Revolution: A Handbook* (New York: HarperBusiness, 1995).

A practical way to prevent people from bringing their bias into the data collection process is to assign people who are not involved in the process on a day-to-day basis. If necessary, the results can then be reviewed by people performing the process.

Good data collection methods and techniques can save a PMT a considerable amount of time and money, but the real payoff is in improving the validity of the project results and the recommendations on which they are based.*

---

*Refer to: Patricia K. Felkins, B. J. Chakiris, and Kenneth N. Chakiris, *Change Management: A Model for Effective Organizational Performance* (White Plains, N.Y.: Quality Resources, 1993), 211–264.

Chapter 9

NVA Dictionary

Purpose

It is worthwhile for the analyst to identify and tag non–value-added actions as early in the as-is diagramming phase as possible so that the results of a detailed analysis can be improved. Non–value actions are those that add no value to the intended stakeholder.

The dictionary contains the NVA actions most frequently used when diagramming and analyzing a process.

The purpose of the dictionary is to provide guidance in evaluating whether the actions used in describing activities in your business processes are potentially non–value-added. The dictionary includes commonly used verbs that describe non–value-added actions in most business processes. It is not intended to be all inclusive, but does includes some commonly used synonyms and related actions.

The 35 verbs, or non–valued-added (NVA) actions, contained in this dictionary came from creating as-is process diagrams for a variety of commercial businesses and governmental organizations over the past five years. The dictionary contains words that are used most frequently in the process analysis phase of a project. The only criterion for including a word in the dictionary is its frequency of occurrence in process analysis work.

Set up, for example, is included because it occurs frequently in a variety of businesses. The rationale for including it in the dictionary is as follows:

The work involved in setting something up (or preparing it) to produce an output of some kind can usually be minimized or eliminated completely without adversely affecting the execution (or production) process itself. As a result, the total cycle time could be reduced significantly which, in the end, benefits stakeholders.

This analysis is relatively consistent from business to business, so *set up* is included in the dictionary.

Dictionary Construction

Word usage   The description of each word is not intended to be a dictionary definition. It only describes the most common usage I found helpful in diagramming business processes.

Diagramming symbol   The ANSI standard symbol assigned to each action is based on its usage. The following symbols are generally used in preparing a process diagram.

- Work step (rectangle)
- Inspection step (ellipse)
- Storage step (inverted triangle)
- Delay step (half sausage)
- Decision step (diamond)*
- Report step (doc-bezier)

NVA category   The NVA category is assigned based on Table 6.1. The category shown for each action is the one most often associated with it when preparing a process diagram.

RAO example   The example shows how the standard symbol works with the resource, action, and object description of the process step. All of the examples used in the dictionary were taken from as-is diagrams created during actual diagramming sessions.

NVA rationale   This is a general explanation of why each verb was classified as a non–value-added action. When designing a new process, they could be eliminated from the process, but if they remain, they will be NVA by definition. The point of understanding NVA actions is to find ways to eliminate them or to minimize them in instances where they cannot be eliminated.

Synonyms   A list of words that can be used in place of the dictionary word without actually changing its meaning or context. Each synonym gives a slightly different shading to the meaning of the action.

---

*A useful convention for indicating decision steps is to place a question mark after the verb: for example, "Engineering manager **approves?** expense report." Any of the actions shown in the NVA dictionary can be changed to a diamond using this convention.

For example, *changes* means to alter, substitute or replace something with something else. In other words, it can be a major change. On the other hand, the synonym *modifies* implies a modest or moderate change. In some instances, additional clarification is provided because the synonym has a precise meaning.

Related actions   A list of actions that are not synonyms, but that are somewhat related in intent. Often, when searching for a specific word to use on the diagram, another one comes to mind. This list is provided as a cross-reference to the cited word.

Analyst notes   The dictionary is meant to be a working document for the analysts' use during a diagramming session. This space is provided for the analysts to write notes about how each word is used in specific environments.

How to Use the Dictionary

Describe action   Determine the verb that best describes the action in the process step being reviewed. Sometimes it may be colloquial to a particular organization. More often than not it will be a commonly used verb.

Look up word   Look to see if the verb used is listed in the dictionary as either an action, synonym, or related action. If it is, then the verb being used can be categorized. At this point, determine if the word being used should be replaced with one of the verbs provided in the dictionary to better describe the action.

If so, replace it. This usually will be the case unless the verb used is commonly understood by everyone in the organization. If the word cannot be found in the dictionary, then determine if the action is value-added or non–value-added using the procedures described in this book.

Extending the NVA Dictionary

Share new non–value-added action definitions with team members.

Space is provided in the dictionary for analysts to add additional words based on their experience in examining business processes. After using the dictionary on several projects, analysts will find that the words take on greater significance by becoming the standard lexicon project team members use when communicating among themselves and with management.

When a new word is added to the dictionary, analysts should share the analysis and reason for including it with other team members. This will encourage everyone to be on the lookout for clues on how to remove non–value-added work from processes.

Adjusts

To change something to make it fit, conform, or suitable for use.

Symbol: Work step (rectangle)

Category: Processing defects

Example:

Trim saw operator
adjusts
trim saw ruler.

Rationale: If the saw is being adjusted to correct the tolerances of the material being trimmed, the material does not conform to standards and adjusting the saw is a non–value-added corrective action.

Synonyms: adapts

Adapts suggests flexibility in modifying something to suit new conditions.

Related actions: accommodates
conforms to

Accommodates implies subordinating something to the needs of another through concessions or compromise. *Conforms to* means to bring into or act in harmony with some standard pattern or principle.

Analyst notes: _____

_____

_____

_____

_____

_____

Approves

To give consent to someone or something as being good or satisfactory.

Symbol:	Work step (rectangle)
Category:	Process control
Example:	

Engineering manager
approves
expense report.

Rationale:	Approving an expense report is an inspection step that does not add value to the process. Sometimes an approval is required by the stakeholder. For example, FDA inspectors must approve meat before it is shipped for distribution to grocery stores. In this case, the term *certifies* could actually replace *approves*, and the action might be considered value-added since it meets a government requirement.
Synonyms:	certifies endorses ratifies
	Certifies implies official approval because of compliance with the requirements or standards. *Endorses* adds the further implication of active support or advocacy. *Ratifies* implies official approval of that which has been done by one's representative.
Related actions:	recommends
	Recommends implies empowerment, commitment, or placing trust in something or someone. It also means that something is favorably suited for some use, function, position, and so on.
Analyst notes:	_____
	_____
	_____
	_____
	_____
	_____

Assigns

To set something apart from something else or mark it for a specific purpose.

Symbol: Work step (rectangle)

Category: Preparation

Example:

Chief draftsperson **assigns** design project.

Rationale: Assigning projects to specific people is probably an unnecessary step because the procedure can usually be replaced by establishing an allocation procedure that the draftspersons follow. For example, a rule that the first available draftsperson takes the oldest project in the queue could be established. As new projects come in they go to the bottom of the pile.

Synonyms: allocates
appoints

Allocates also suggests setting something apart for a specific purpose or in accordance with a plan. *Appoints* implies an official act of assignment to a position or an office.

Related actions: consigns
designates
distributes

Consigns implies handing over, giving up, or delivering something. *Designates* means to point out, mark out, indicate, or specify something. *Distributes* implies dividing and giving out in shares or according to a classification.

Analyst notes: _____

_____

_____

_____

_____

_____

Changes

To alter, substitute, or replace something with something else.

Symbol: Work step (rectangle)

Category: Processing defects

Example:

> Production scheduler
> **changes**
> production schedule.

Rationale: Change generally results from problems earlier in the
process that are caught during inspection or as a request
from customers. The general rule is: Do the right thing
right the first time.

Synonyms: adjusts
alters
corrects
modifies

Adjusts is to make something fit, conform, or suitable for
use. *Alters* implies a partial change, as in appearance. *Corrects* implies to make right a wrong or error. *Modifies* implies minor change, often so as to limit or moderate.

Related actions: converts
conforms to
edits
revises

Converts implies a change to suit a new function or a new
requirement. *Conforms to* means to bring into or act in
harmony with some standard pattern, principle, and so on.
Edits mean to revise and make ready for publication. *Revises* is to correct, improve, or update where necessary.

Analyst notes: _____

_____

_____

_____

Collates

To put something in its proper order.

Symbol: Work step (rectangle)

Category: Movement and handling

Example:

```
                    ┌─────────────────┐
              ──────▶│  Sales secretary │──────▶
                    │     collates     │
                    │   sales reports. │
                    └─────────────────┘
```

Rationale: Collating is a step that can ususally be eliminated through improved scheduling or the better use of technology. For example, this step can be eliminated with a copier that has collating capability.

Synonyms: separates
                    sorts

                    Separates means to set or put apart into sections, groups, sets, or units. *Sorts* implies placing, separating, or arranging according to class or kind.

Related actions: compares
                     organizes

                    Compares means to examine in order to observe or discover similarities or differences. *Organizes* implies that arranging of things is done in an orderly way.

Analyst notes: _____

                    _____

                    _____

                    _____

                    _____

                    _____

Collects

To gather things together for some purpose.

Symbol: Work step (rectangle)

Category: Movement and handling

Example:

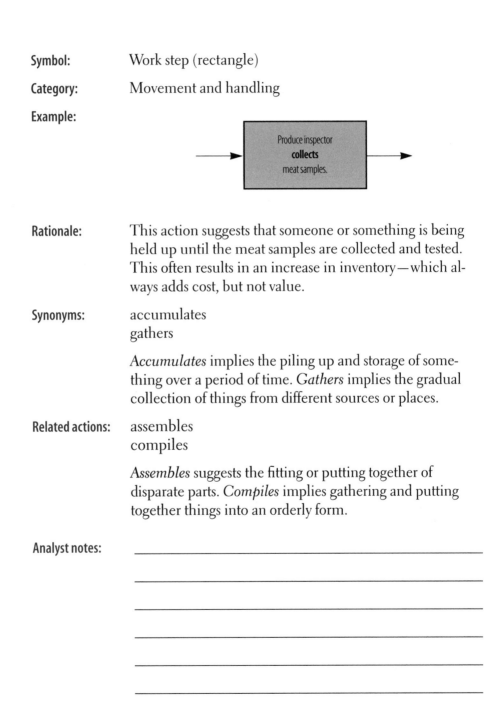

Produce inspector
collects
meat samples.

Rationale: This action suggests that someone or something is being held up until the meat samples are collected and tested. This often results in an increase in inventory—which always adds cost, but not value.

Synonyms: accumulates
gathers

Accumulates implies the piling up and storage of something over a period of time. *Gathers* implies the gradual collection of things from different sources or places.

Related actions: assembles
compiles

Assembles suggests the fitting or putting together of disparate parts. *Compiles* implies gathering and putting together things into an orderly form.

Analyst notes: _____

_____

_____

_____

_____

_____

Copies

To make an imitation of an original thing.

Symbol: Work step (rectangle)

Category: Movement and handling

Example:

Accounting clerk
copies
supplier invoice.

Rationale: Either the number of copies needed has not been properly specified or the invoice has an error. If the invoice was prepared correctly in the first place or the number of copies properly specified, then this step would not be necessary.

Synonyms: duplicates
                     reproduces

Duplicates implies a double, or counterpart of something, all serving the purposes of the original. *Reproduces* implies a close imitation of the original, often, however, with differences, as of material, size, or quality.

Related actions: transcribes

Transcribes means to write out or type out in full.

Analyst notes: _____

_____

_____

_____

_____

_____

Delivers

To carry something and leave it at the proper place or places.

Symbol: Work step (rectangle)

Category: Movement and handling

Example:

Rationale: The act of physically delivering something does not in-
                     crease its value. It is not always possible to eliminate this
                     step; however, every effort should be made to reduce the
                     time and cost to perform it. In the example, this time and
                     cost might be reduced by having the sales report electroni-
                     cally distributed rather than physically distributed by the
                     sales secretary.

Synonyms: distributes
                     transfers

                     Distributes implies putting things in various distinct places.
                     Transfers implies conveying, carrying, removing, or send-
                     ing from one place or position to another.

Related actions: issues

                     Issues implies sending out or putting forth.

Analyst notes: _____

                     _____

                     _____

                     _____

                     _____

                     _____

Distributes

To give something out, scatter it, or spread it out.

Symbol: Work step (rectangle)

Category: Movement and handling

Example:

Payroll clerk
distributes
weekly paychecks.

Rationale: Distributing something typically does not add value to the
                     product or service provided to the customer. In this case,
                     distribute *may* be performed for business or regulatory
                     purposes; however, arranging direct deposit to the employ-
                     ees' bank accounts would be much more efficient.

Synonyms: issues

                     Issues implies sending out or putting forth.

Related actions: faxes
                     mails
                     sends

                     Faxes implies sending by electronic means an exact repro-
                     duction or copy. *Mails* is to send by mail, as by putting into
                     a mailbox or the postal system. *Sends* implies dispatching,
                     conveying, or transmitting.

Analyst notes: _____

                     _____

                     _____

                     _____

                     _____

                     _____

Eliminates

To take someone or something out; remove it or get rid of it.

Symbol:	Work step (rectangle)
Category:	Processing waste
Example:	

> Product inspector
> **eliminates**
> impure chemicals.

Rationale:	Processing waste is a step that is unnecessary if ways can be devised to ensure that the contamination doesn't occur in the first place.
Synonyms:	removes
	Removes implies doing away with something.
Related actions:	cancels
	disposes of
	Cancels implies doing away with, wiping out, or abolishing something. *Disposes of* implies getting rid of or throwing something away.
Analyst notes:	

Expedites

To speed something up or make the progress of it easier.

Symbol: Work step (rectangle)

Category: Process control

Example:

```
               ┌─────────────────────┐
               │  Production expediter │
  ────────────▶│      expedites        │────────▶
               │    overdue orders.    │
               └─────────────────────┘
```

Rationale: Expediting is required when schedules are not being met or when a customer requests shipment sooner than originally requested. In either case the act adds cost, but not value, unless the customer is willing to pay for the change or trades for future business.

Synonyms: facilitates

Facilitates implies making something easier.

Related actions: coordinates
dispatches

Coordinates implies bringing something into a proper order or relation, or adjusting so as to have harmonious action. *Dispatches* implies the removing of impediments.

Analyst notes: _____

_____

_____

_____

_____

_____

Files

To arrange something in order for future reference or to put it in its proper place or order.

Symbol: Storage step (inverted triangle)

Category: Storage

Example:

Correspondent **files** customer orders.

Rationale: Filing is a non–value-added activity because it is usually done for reference purposes—usually to correct problems that crop up after a transaction is completed. A study of real estate records disclosed that only 2 percent of documents are used more than once.

Synonyms: catalogs
                   classifies

                   Catalogs implies including something in a complete and extensive list. *Classifies* implies arranging or grouping things in classes according to some system or principle.

Related actions: deposits
                      records

                      Deposits implies placing something for safekeeping. *Records* implies putting in writing for future use.

Analyst notes: _____

                     _____

                     _____

                     _____

                     _____

                     _____

Identifies

To recognize someone or something as being the person or thing known, described, or claimed.

Symbol: Inspection step (ellipse)

Category: Process control

Example:

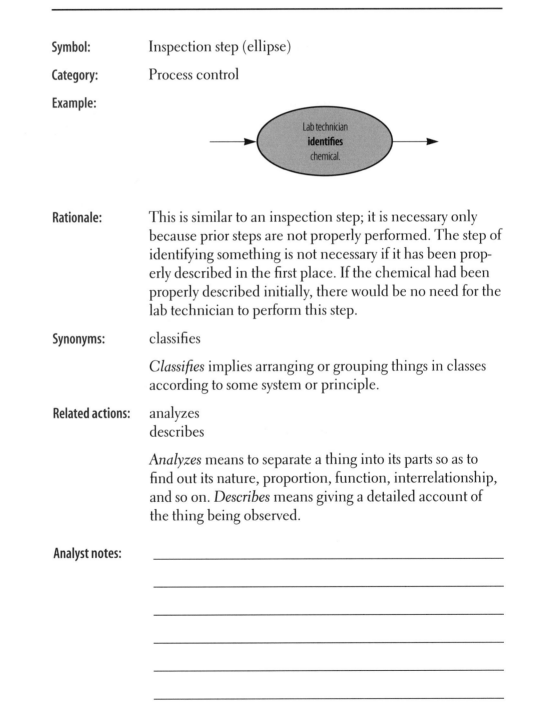

Lab technician
identifies
chemical.

Rationale: This is similar to an inspection step; it is necessary only because prior steps are not properly performed. The step of identifying something is not necessary if it has been properly described in the first place. If the chemical had been properly described initially, there would be no need for the lab technician to perform this step.

Synonyms: classifies

Classifies implies arranging or grouping things in classes according to some system or principle.

Related actions: analyzes
describes

Analyzes means to separate a thing into its parts so as to find out its nature, proportion, function, interrelationship, and so on. *Describes* means giving a detailed account of the thing being observed.

Analyst notes: _____

_____

_____

_____

_____

_____

_____

Inspects

To look at something carefully or examine it critically in order to detect flaws or errors.

Symbol: Inspection step (ellipse)

Category: Process control

Example:

Quality technician
inspects
laminate surface.

Rationale: Inspection is typically performed to identify and eliminate defective work. Even if the inspection is done at the customer's request or is required by a regulatory agency to document proof of compliance, it does not add value to the product or service.

Synonyms: audits
checks
tests
verifies

Audits implies a formal and thorough examination and evaluation. *Checks* means to test, compare, or examine. *Tests* means an examination, experiment, or trial. *Verifies* means to prove something to be true by demonstration, evidence, or testimony.

Related actions: examines
investigates
searches for

Examines means to look at something critically or methodically in order to find out facts and conditions. *Investigates* means to search into something so as to learn the facts. *Searches for* means to review something for the purpose of finding an object or fact.

Analyst notes: _____

_____

_____

Issues

To print or publish something publicly or officially.

Symbol: Work step (rectangle)

Category: Movement and handling

Example:

Sales manager
issues
sales policy.

Rationale: Issuing a sales policy does not add any value to the process unless it is understood, used, and followed by everyone affected. Issuing the policy does not ensure that it will be followed.

Synonyms: distributes

Distributes implies putting things in various distinct places.

Related actions: delivers
publishes

Delivers means to carry something and leave it at the proper place or places. *Publishes* suggests making publicly known a written work.

Analyst notes: _____

_____

_____

_____

_____

_____

Labels

To attach a card or strip of paper to an object to indicate its nature, contents, ownership, or destination.

Symbol: Work step (rectangle)

Category: Process control

Example:

Shipping clerk
labels
product container.

Rationale: Labeling the shipping container is done as a process control to record what was shipped, in case there is an error later on. Even if the label is a regulatory requirement, it does not add value. If it is the *only* way to make sure the right product gets to the customer, it may be considered value-added—but a different verb (*addresses*) should probably be used.

Synonyms: marks
tags

Marks means placing a visible object of known position, indicating, among other things, ownership, standard of quality, and similar information. *Tags* suggests a card, ticket, plastic marker, or similar device tied or attached to something for identification.

Related actions: records

Records implies putting in writing for future use.

Analyst notes: _____

_____

_____

_____

_____

_____

Loads

To put someone or something into or on something else.

Symbol: Work step (rectangle)

Category: Movement and handling

Example:

Material handler
loads
delivery truck.

Rationale: Loads is necessary to transport the goods to customers, but it does not add value to the product. This action may not be totally eliminated, but the time and cost required to perform the task can usually be reduced significantly.

Synonyms: fills

Fills implies putting a considerable quantity of something into a receptacle until it is full.

Related actions: accumulates
stacks

Accumulates implies the piling up of things over a period of time. *Stacks* suggests an orderly pile or heap.

Analyst notes: _____

_____

_____

_____

_____

_____

Maintains

To keep something in a good condition, position, or repair.

Symbol:	Work step (rectangle)
Category:	Processing defects
Example:	

Service technician **maintains** copier.

Rationale: Maintaining the copier is usually necessary for it to continue to make quality copies. But maintaining it does not increase its value for making copies, however, it does add to its cost.

Synonyms: cleans
repairs

Cleans suggests the removing of dirt or other impurities. *Repairs* means to put back in good condition after damage, decay, and so on.

Related actions: fixes

Fixes means to restore to proper condition.

Analyst notes: _____

_____

_____

_____

_____

_____

Measures

To determine or estimate the dimensions of something by the use of a standard.

Symbol: Work step (rectangle)

Category: Process control

Example:

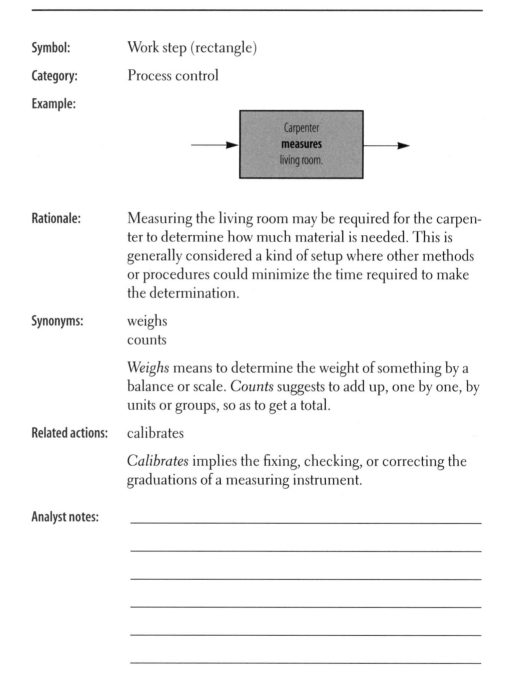

Carpenter
measures
living room.

Rationale: Measuring the living room may be required for the carpenter to determine how much material is needed. This is generally considered a kind of setup where other methods or procedures could minimize the time required to make the determination.

Synonyms: weighs
counts

Weighs means to determine the weight of something by a balance or scale. *Counts* suggests to add up, one by one, by units or groups, so as to get a total.

Related actions: calibrates

Calibrates implies the fixing, checking, or correcting the graduations of a measuring instrument.

Analyst notes: _____

_____

_____

_____

_____

_____

Monitors

To check on or regulate the performance of someone or something.

Symbol:	Inspection step (ellipse)
Category:	Process control
Example:	

Treater operator
monitors
oven temperature.

Rationale: Monitoring the oven temperature suggests that variations could occur that would lead to deviations that unfavorably affect the output. The operator is responsible for catching the deviation before an unfavorable event occurs. Excessive variation can usually be eliminated by improving the equipment design, changing the materials used, or developing better procedures.

Synonyms: observes
regulates
supervises

Observes implies paying special attention to something. *Regulates* suggests controlling, directing, or governing according to a rule, principle, or system. *Supervises* means to oversee, direct, or manage something.

Related actions: controls

Controls suggests verifying something by comparing to a standard.

Analyst notes: _____

_____

_____

_____

_____

_____

Moves

To change the place or position of something by pushing, carrying, or pulling it from one place or position to another.

Symbol: Work step (rectangle)

Category: Movement and handling

Example:

```
              ┌─────────────────────┐
              │   Material handler   │
     ────────►│       moves          │────────►
              │     empty drums.     │
              └─────────────────────┘
```

Rationale: Changing the location of the empty drums does not increase their value. Improving material handling and storage procedures can usually eliminate such unnecessary steps.

Synonyms: pushes
                     pulls
                     carries

                     Pushes implies exerting force or pressure against something so as to move it. *Pulls* means to exert force or influence on something to cause it to move toward or after the source of the force. *Carries* means to hold something while moving it.

Related actions: retrieves
                     sends
                     transmits

                     Retrieves means to get something back. *Sends* means to cause to go or be carried. *Transmits* implies sending or causing to go from one place to another across intervening space or distance.

Analyst notes: _____

                     _____

                     _____

                     _____

                     _____

Receives

To take or get something given, offered, or sent by someone or something.

Symbol:	Work step (rectangle)
Category:	Movement and handling
Example:	

> Salesperson
> **receives**
> customer order.

Rationale: Receiving something is a passive action that is performed in response to an output from a prior step. It neither adds value nor detracts from value. The step may not require elimination, but the way it is accomplished should be made as simple as possible.

Synonyms: admits

Admits stresses permission or concession on the part of the person who receives something.

Related actions: accepts
acquires
obtains
takes

Accepts means to receive willingly or favorably, but it sometimes connotes acquiescence rather than explicit approval. *Acquires* means to get by one's own efforts or actions. *Obtains* means to get possession of something by some effort. *Takes,* in this connection, means to accept something offered or presented.

Analyst notes: _____

_____

_____

_____

_____

_____

Reconciles

To make arguments, ideas, texts, or accounts of something consistent and compatible with something else.

Symbol: Work step (rectangle)

Category: Processing defects

Example:

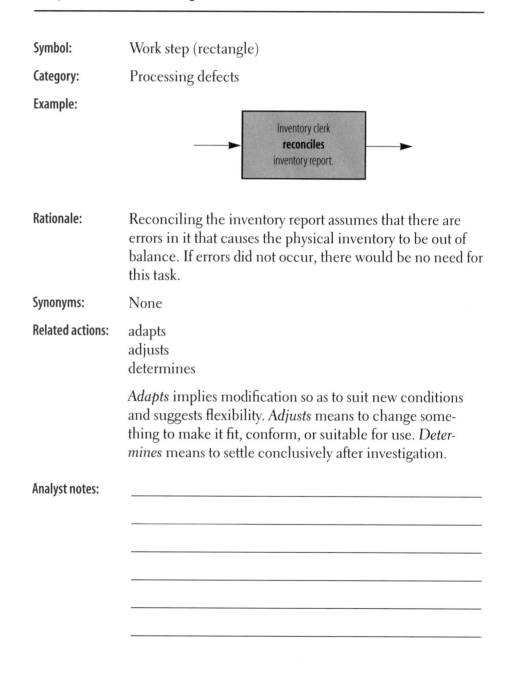

Inventory clerk
reconciles
inventory report.

Rationale: Reconciling the inventory report assumes that there are errors in it that causes the physical inventory to be out of balance. If errors did not occur, there would be no need for this task.

Synonyms: None

Related actions: adapts
                   adjusts
                   determines

                   Adapts implies modification so as to suit new conditions and suggests flexibility. *Adjusts* means to change something to make it fit, conform, or suitable for use. *Determines* means to settle conclusively after investigation.

Analyst notes: _____

                   _____

                   _____

                   _____

                   _____

                   _____

Records

To put something into writing for future use.

Symbol: Work step (rectangle)

Category: Process control

Example:

Rationale: Recording the inventory count does not add value to the products in inventory. Recording is a process control step that checks to make sure that the inventory records are in agreement with the actual inventory count.

Synonyms: documents

Documents means to provide written proof.

Related actions:
enters
files
inputs
labels
posts
transcribes

Enters means to write down in a record, list, diary, and so on. *Files* means to arrange something in order for future reference or to put it in its proper place or order. *Inputs* means the act of putting in. *Labels* means to attach a card or strip of paper to an object to indicate its nature, contents, ownership, or destination. *Posts* means to enter all necessary items in the correct form and place. *Transcribes* means to write out or type out in full.

Analyst notes: _____

_____

_____

_____

_____

Repairs

To put something back in good condition after damage or decay.

Symbol: Work step (rectangle)

Category: Processing defects

Example:

Rationale: Repairing fuel oil that has become oxidized over time is restoring it to its original state. This is an additional cost that must be absorbed as a result of improper storage.

Synonyms: fixes
                     reworks

Fixes means to restore to proper condition. *Reworks* implies that some or all of the original steps in producing a product or service must be repeated.

Related actions: changes
                     maintains
                     revises

Changes means to alter, substitute, or replace something with something else. *Maintains* means to keep something in a good condition, position, or repair. *Revises* means to read something over carefully and correct, improve, or update it where necessary.

Analyst notes: _____

                     _____

                     _____

                     _____

                     _____

                     _____

Requests

To express a wish or desire for something in a polite or formal way.

Symbol: Work step (rectangle)

Category: Preparation

Example:

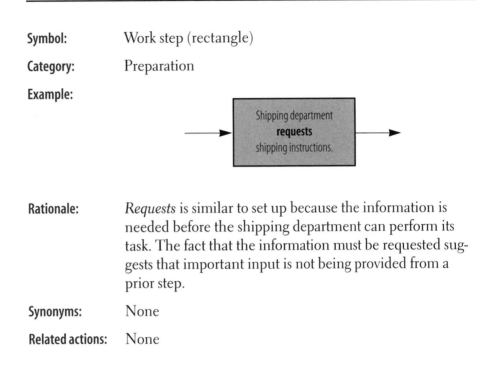

Rationale: *Requests* is similar to set up because the information is needed before the shipping department can perform its task. The fact that the information must be requested suggests that important input is not being provided from a prior step.

Synonyms: None

Related actions: None

Analyst notes: _____

                       _____

                       _____

                       _____

                       _____

                       _____

Returns

To bring, send, carry, or put something back.

Symbol: Work step (rectangle)

Category: Processing defects

Example:

Rationale: The prefix *re* implies that something is being done over or reversed. In either case it reduces the value of whatever is being returned. For instance, a customer returning defective product certainly does not provide value to either the customer or the supplier.

Synonyms: restores
                     refunds

                     Restores means to bring back to a former or normal condition. *Refunds* implies giving back or repaying funds.

Related actions: replaces

                     Replaces means to provide a substitute or equivalent for something.

Analyst notes: _____

                     _____

                     _____

                     _____

                     _____

                     _____

Reviews

To examine or inspect something formally.

Symbol: Inspection step (ellipse)

Category: Process control

Example:

Shop supervisor **reviews** process output.

Rationale: Reviews is an inspection step that checks for errors, defects, or incorrect information. If the process output was errorless or defect free, then this step would be unnecessary.

Synonyms: audits
analyzes
examines
inspects

Audits implies a formal and thorough examination and evaluation. *Analyzes* means to separate a thing into its parts so as to find out its nature, proportion, function, interrelationship, and so on. *Examines* means to look at or into something critically or methodically. *Inspects* means to look at something carefully or examine it critically.

Related actions: checks
investigates
tests
verifies

Checks means to test, compare, and examine to determine if something is as it should be. *Investigates* means to search into something so as to learn the facts. *Tests* means an examination, experiment, or trial. *Verifies* means to prove something to be true by demonstration, evidence, or testimony.

Analyst notes: _____

_____

_____

Revises

To read something over carefully and to correct, improve, or update it where necessary.

Symbol: Work step (rectangle)

Category: Processing defects

Example:

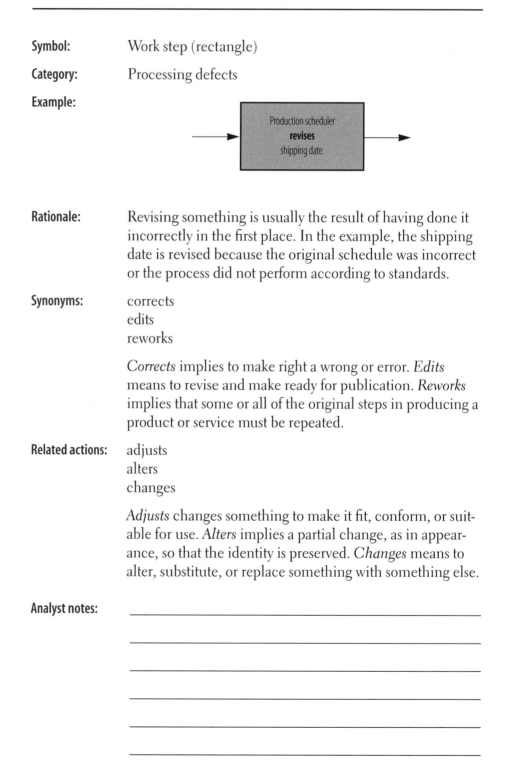

Production scheduler
revises
shipping date.

Rationale: Revising something is usually the result of having done it incorrectly in the first place. In the example, the shipping date is revised because the original schedule was incorrect or the process did not perform according to standards.

Synonyms: corrects
                     edits
                     reworks

                     Corrects implies to make right a wrong or error. *Edits* means to revise and make ready for publication. *Reworks* implies that some or all of the original steps in producing a product or service must be repeated.

Related actions: adjusts
                     alters
                     changes

                     Adjusts changes something to make it fit, conform, or suitable for use. *Alters* implies a partial change, as in appearance, so that the identity is preserved. *Changes* means to alter, substitute, or replace something with something else.

Analyst notes: _____

                     _____

                     _____

                     _____

                     _____

                     _____

Selects

To choose or pick something from among several alternatives.

Symbol: Work step (rectangle)

Category: Process control

Example:

Purchasing agent
selects
steel supplier.

Rationale: *Selects* is similar to an inspection process as a choice is made among alternatives based upon some predetermined criteria. If suppliers are already prequalified then the process could be automated, eliminating the need for this step.

Synonyms: chooses

                     Chooses means to pick out by preference from what is available.

Related actions: None

Analyst notes: _____

                     _____

                     _____

                     _____

                     _____

                     _____

Sets Up

To prepare something for future use.

Symbol: Work step (rectangle)

Category: Preparation

Example:

```
                    Machine operator
              →         sets up           →
                          lathe.
```

Rationale: Setting up a lathe does not produce the product. The actual operation of the lathe is what produces product. Although the setup step cannot be entirely eliminated, every effort to minimize the setup cycle time should be made, as it reduces costs and improves process flexibility.

Synonyms: establishes

                       Establishes means to set up.

Related actions: arranges
                       organizes
                       prepares

                       Arranges means to put in the correct, proper, or suitable order. *Organizes* implies that arranging of things is done in an orderly way. *Prepares* means to make ready or suitable, usually for a specific purpose.

Analyst notes: _____

                       _____

                       _____

                       _____

                       _____

                       _____

Stages

To stop something on its journey through a process and hold it in a particular place.

Symbol: Work step (rectangle)

Category: Preparation

Example:

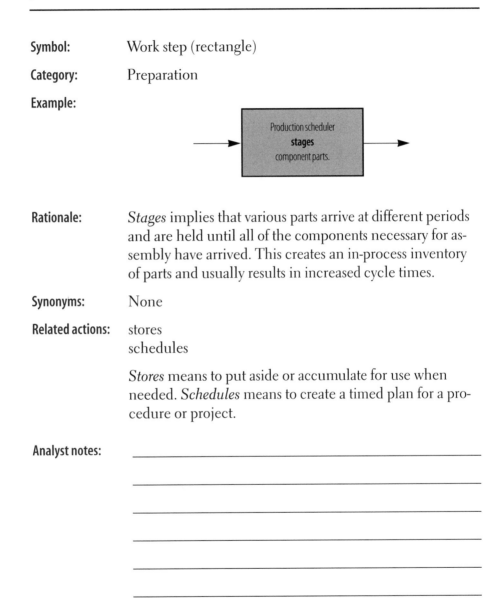

Rationale: *Stages* implies that various parts arrive at different periods and are held until all of the components necessary for assembly have arrived. This creates an in-process inventory of parts and usually results in increased cycle times.

Synonyms: None

Related actions: stores
schedules

Stores means to put aside or accumulate for use when needed. *Schedules* means to create a timed plan for a procedure or project.

Analyst notes: _____

_____

_____

_____

_____

_____

Updates

To bring something up to date or make it conform to the most recent facts, methods, or ideas.

Symbol: Work step (rectangle)

Category: Storage

Example:

Production scheduler
updates
production schedule.

Rationale: In the example, the production schedule is updated as actual versus planned production is reported. The changes are required as a result of not producing as planned. This activity is not producing any new value, but rather correcting for variation.

Synonyms: edits

Edits means to revise and make ready for publication.

Related actions: recreates
restores

Recreates means to restore, refresh, or create anew. Restores means to bring back to a former or normal condition.

Analyst notes: _____

_____

_____

_____

_____

_____

Verifies

To test or check the accuracy or correctness of something through investigation, comparison with a standard, or reference to the facts.

Symbol:	Inspection step (ellipse)
Category:	Process control
Example:	

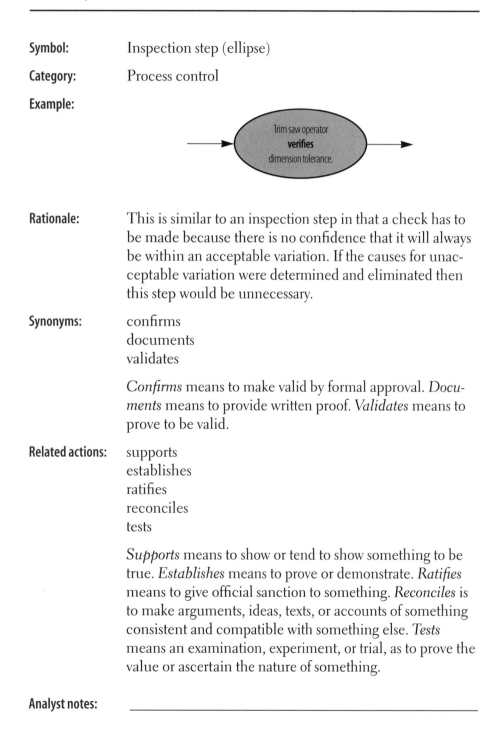

Rationale: This is similar to an inspection step in that a check has to be made because there is no confidence that it will always be within an acceptable variation. If the causes for unacceptable variation were determined and eliminated then this step would be unnecessary.

Synonyms: confirms
documents
validates

Confirms means to make valid by formal approval. *Documents* means to provide written proof. *Validates* means to prove to be valid.

Related actions: supports
establishes
ratifies
reconciles
tests

Supports means to show or tend to show something to be true. *Establishes* means to prove or demonstrate. *Ratifies* means to give official sanction to something. *Reconciles* is to make arguments, ideas, texts, or accounts of something consistent and compatible with something else. *Tests* means an examination, experiment, or trial, as to prove the value or ascertain the nature of something.

Analyst notes: _____

_____

Waits For

To stop and wait for someone or something to catch up.

Symbol: Delay step (half-sausage)

Category: Movement and handling

Example:

Doctor
waits for
test results.

Rationale: Waiting for any output is a non–value-added activity. Certainly, waiting for test results so that a diagnosis can be made, and remedial action taken, is not of value to the doctor or the patient.

Synonyms: delays
pauses for

Delays means to make later; slow up action. *Pauses for* implies a short period of inaction, temporary stop, or break.

Related actions: halts
stops

Halts means to stop temporarily. *Stops* means to prevent the movement or further movement of something.

Analyst notes: _____

_____

_____

_____

_____

_____

Alphabetical List of Actions

#	Action	Assessment	Symbol	Category
1	Accommodates	Non–value-added	Rectangle	Processing defects
2	Adapts	Non–value-added	Rectangle	Processing defects
3	Adjusts	Non–value-added	Rectangle	Processing defects
4	Administers	Non–value-added	Rectangle	Process control
5	Admits	Non–value-added	Rectangle	Movement and handling
6	Allocates	Non–value-added	Rectangle	Preparation
7	Alters	Non–value-added	Rectangle	Processing defects
8	Analyzes	Non–value-added	Ellipse	Process control
9	Appoints	Non–value-added	Rectangle	Preparation
10	Approves	Non–value-added	Rectangle	Process control
11	Assembles	Value-added	Rectangle	Execution
12	Assigns	Non–value-added	Rectangle	Preparation
13	Audits	Non–value-added	Rectangle	Process control
14	Calculates	Value-added	Rectangle	Execution
15	Calibrates	Non–value-added	Rectangle	Process control
16	Carries	Non–value-added	Rectangle	Movement and handling
17	Catalogs	Non–value-added	Inverted triangle	Storage
18	Certifies	Non–value-added	Rectangle	Process control
19	Changes	Non–value-added	Rectangle	Processing defects
20	Checks	Non–value-added	Ellipse	Process control
21	Chooses	Non–value-added	Rectangle	Process control
22	Classifies	Non–value-added	Rectangle	Movement and handling

Actions in rose are included in the NVA dictionary.

#	Action	Assessment	Symbol	Category
23	Cleans	Non–value-added	Rectangle	Processing defects
24	Collates	Non–value-added	Rectangle	Movement and handling
25	Collects	Non–value-added	Rectangle	Movement and handling
26	Completes	Value-added	Rectangle	Execution
27	Confirms	Non–value-added	Rectangle	Process control
28	Copies	Non–value-added	Rectangle	Movement and handling
29	Corrects	Non–value-added	Rectangle	Processing defects
30	Counts	Non–value-added	Rectangle	Process control
31	Creates	Value-added	Rectangle	Execution
32	Defines	Value-added	Rectangle	Execution
33	Delays	Non–value-added	Inverted triangle	Storage
34	Delivers	Non–value-added	Rectangle	Movement and handling
35	Deploys	Value-added	Rectangle	Execution
36	Designs	Value-added	Rectangle	Execution
37	Determines	Value-added	Rectangle	Execution
38	Develops	Value-added	Rectangle	Execution
39	Distributes	Non–value-added	Rectangle	Movement and handling
40	Eliminates	Non–value-added	Rectangle	Processing waste
41	Endorses	Non–value-added	Rectangle	Process control
42	Establishes	Non–value-added	Rectangle	Preparation
43	Examines	Non–value-added	Ellipse	Process control
44	Executes	Value-added	Rectangle	Execution
45	Expedites	Non–value-added	Rectangle	Process control
46	Fabricates	Value-added	Rectangle	Execution
47	Facilitates	Non–value-added	Rectangle	Process control
48	Files	Non–value-added	Inverted triangle	Storage
49	Fills	Non–value-added	Rectangle	Movement and handling
50	Fixes	Non–value-added	Rectangle	Processing defects
51	Formulates	Value-added	Rectangle	Planning
52	Gathers	Non–value-added	Rectangle	Movement and handling
53	Identifies	Non–value-added	Ellipse	Process control
54	Implements	Value-added	Rectangle	Execution
55	Inspects	Non–value-added	Ellipse	Process control

Actions in rose are included in the NVA dictionary.

#	Action	Assessment	Symbol	Category
56	Installs	Value-added	Rectangle	Execution
57	Integrates	Value-added	Rectangle	Execution
58	Issues	Non-value-added	Rectangle	Movement and handling
59	Labels	Non-value-added	Rectangle	Process control
60	Loads	Non-value-added	Rectangle	Movement and handling
61	Maintains	Non-value-added	Rectangle	Processing defects
62	Manages	Value-added	Rectangle	Prevention
63	Marks	Non-value-added	Rectangle	Process control
64	Measures	Non-value-added	Rectangle	Process control
65	Modifies	Non-value-added	Rectangle	Processing defects
66	Monitors	Non-value-added	Ellipse	Process control
67	Moves	Non-value-added	Rectangle	Movement and handling
68	Negotiates	Value-added	Rectangle	Planning
69	Observes	Non-value-added	Ellipse	Process control
70	Pauses for	Non-value-added	Half sausage	Storage
71	Plans	Value-added	Rectangle	Planning
72	Presents	Value-added	Rectangle	Planning
73	Prioritizes	Value-added	Rectangle	Planning
74	Processes	Value-added	Rectangle	Execution
75	Produces	Value-added	Rectangle	Execution
76	Provides	Value-added	Rectangle	Execution
77	Pulls	Non-value-added	Rectangle	Movement and handling
78	Pushes	Non-value-added	Rectangle	Movement and handling
79	Ratifies	Non-value-added	Rectangle	Process control
80	Receives	Non-value-added	Rectangle	Movement and handling
81	Reconciles	Non-value-added	Rectangle	Processing defects
82	Records	Non-value-added	Rectangle	Process control
83	Refunds	Non-value-added	Rectangle	Processing defects
84	Regulates	Non-value-added	Ellipse	Process control
85	Removes	Non-value-added	Rectangle	Processing waste
86	Repairs	Non-value-added	Rectangle	Processing defects
87	Reports	Value-added	Rectangle	Process control
88	Reproduces	Non-value-added	Rectangle	Movement and handling

Actions in rose are included in the NVA dictionary.

#	Action	Assessment	Symbol	Category
89	Requests	Non–value-added	Rectangle	Preparation
90	Restores	Non–value-added	Rectangle	Processing defects
91	Returns	Non–value-added	Rectangle	Processing defects
92	Reviews	Non–value-added	Ellipse	Process control
93	Revises	Non–value-added	Rectangle	Processing defects
94	Reworks	Non–value-added	Rectangle	Processing defects
95	Selects	Non–value-added	Rectangle	Process control
96	Separates	Non–value-added	Rectangle	Movement and handling
97	Sets up	Non–value-added	Rectangle	Preparation
98	Sorts	Non–value-added	Rectangle	Movement and handling
99	Stages	Non–value-added	Rectangle	Preparation
100	Stores	Non–value-added	Inverted triangle	Storage
101	Tags	Non–value-added	Rectangle	Process control
102	Tests	Non–value-added	Ellipse	Process control
103	Transfers	Non–value-added	Rectangle	Movement and handling
104	Updates	Non–value-added	Rectangle	Process control
105	Validates	Non–value-added	Rectangle	Process control
106	Verifies	Non–value-added	Ellipse	Process control
107	Waits for	Non–value-added	Half sausage	Storage
108	Weighs	Non–value-added	Rectangle	Process control

Actions in rose are included in the NVA dictionary.

Additional Reading

Organizational Change

Felkins, Patricia K., B. J. Chakiris, and Kenneth N. Chakiris. *Change Management: A Model for Effective Organizational Performance*. New York: Quality Resources, 1993.

Gardfield, C. A. *Second to None: How Our Smartest Companies Put People First*. Homewood, Ill.: Business One Irwin, 1992.

Kanter, R. M. *The Change Masters: Innovations for Productivity in the American Corporation*. New York: Simon and Schuster, 1983.

Keidel, R. W. *Corporate Players: Designs for Working and Winning Together*. New York: John Wiley & Sons, 1988.

Martel, L. *Mastering Change: The Key to Business Success*. New York: Simon & Schuster, 1986.

Naisbitt, J., and P. Aburdene. *Re-inventing the Corporation: Transforming Your Job and Your Company for the New Informational Society*. New York: Warner Books, 1985.

Senge, Peter. *The Fifth Discipline: The Art and Practice of The Learning Organization*. New York: Doubleday, 1990.

Strategic Planning

Hanan, M. *Tomorrow's Competition: The Next Generation of Growth Strategies*. New York: AMACOM, 1991.

Olins, W. *Corporate Identity: Making Business Strategy Visible Through Design*. Boston: Harvard Business School Press, 1989.

Steiner, G. A. *Strategic Planning: What Every Manager Must Know.* New York: Free Press, 1979.

Waterman, R. H. *The Renewal Factor: How the Best Get and Keep the Competitive Edge.* Toronto and New York: Bantam Books, 1987.

Zachman, J. W. "Developing and Executing Business Strategies Using Process Quality, Management." Paper presented at IMPRO 90, Walton, Conn., 1989.

Process Management

Brassard, M. *The Memory Jogger Plus.* Methuen, Mass.: Goal/QPC, 1989.

Chomsky, Noam. *Language and Problems of Knowledge: The Managua Lectures.* Cambridge, Mass.: MIT Press, 1988.

DeRose, Louis J. *The Value Network: Integrating the Five Critical Processes That Create Customer Satisfaction.* New York: AMACOM, 1994.

Harshbarger, R. *Process Analysis Technique.* Chicago: Macmillan–McGraw-Hill, 1988.

King, R. "Listening to the Voice of the Customer: Using Quality Function Deployment Systems." *National Productivity Review* 6 (summer 1987): 277–281.

Melan, E. H. "Focus on the Process: Key to Quality Improvement." Paper presented at ASQC's 42nd Annual Quality Congress, Dallas, Tex., 1988.

———. *Process Management: Methods for Improving Products and Services.* Milwaukee: ASQC Quality Press; New York: McGraw-Hill, 1993.

———. "Process Management: A Unifying Framework for Improvement." *National Productivity Review* 8, no. 4 (autumn 1989).

Project Management

Adair, Charlene B., and Bruce A. Murray. *Breakthrough Process Redesign: New Pathways to Customers Value.* New York: AMACOM, 1994.

Dinsmore, Paul C. *Human Factors in Project Management.* New York: AMACOM, 1990.

Meredith, Jack R., and Samuel J. Mantel. *Project Management: A Managerial Approach.* 2d ed. New York: John Wiley & Sons, 1989.

Thamhain, H. J., and D. L. Wilemon. "Leadership, Conflict, and Project Management Effectiveness." *Sloan Management Review* 19 (1975): 31–50.

Process Improvement

Davenport, Thomas M. *Process Innovation: Reengineering Work through Information Technology.* Boston, Mass: Harvard Business School Press, 1993.

Hakes, Chris, ed. *Total Quality Management: The Key to Business Improvement.* London: Chapman and Hall, 1991.

Hammer, Michael. "Reengineering Work: Don't Automate, Obliterate." *Harvard Business Review* 68 (July-August 1990): 104–112.

Hammer, Michael, and James A. Champy. *Reengineering the Corporation: A Manifesto for Business Revolution.* New York: HarperBusiness, 1993.

Hammer, Michael, and Steven A. Stanton. *The Reengineering Revolution: A Handbook.* New York: HarperBusiness, 1995.

Harrington, H. J. *Business Process Improvement: The Breakthrough Strategy for Total Quality, Productivity and Competitiveness.* New York: McGraw-Hill, 1991.

Kreigel, Robert J., and Louis Pader. *If it Ain't Broke . . . Break It!* New York: Warner Books, 1992.

Schnitt, David L. "Reengineering the Organization Using Information Technology." *Journal of Systems Management* 44 (January 1993): 14–20.

Stewart, Thomas A. "Reengineering: The Hot New Managing Tool." *Fortune* 128 (23 August 1993): 41–48.

Suzaki, Kiyoshi. *The New Manufacturing Challenge: Techniques for Continuous Improvement.* New York: Free Press, 1987.

Wilder, Clifton. "Measuring the Payoff from Re-engineering." *Computerworld,* 18 November 1991, 65.

Quality Management

Blackbum, Joseph D. "Time-Based Competition: White-Collar Activities." *Business Horizons* 35 (July-August 1992): 96–101.

Grant, Eugene L., and Richard S. Leavenworth. *Statistical Quality Control.* 6th ed. New York: McGraw-Hill, 1988.

Guinta, Lawrence R., and Nancy C. Praizler. *The QFD Book: The Team Approach to Solving Problems and Satisfying Customers through Quality Function Deployment.* New York: AMACOM, 1993.

Index